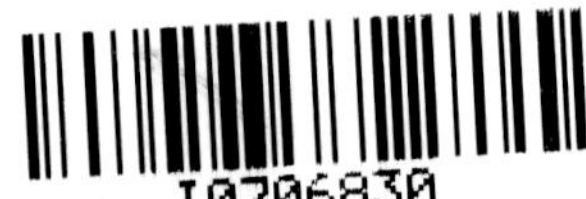

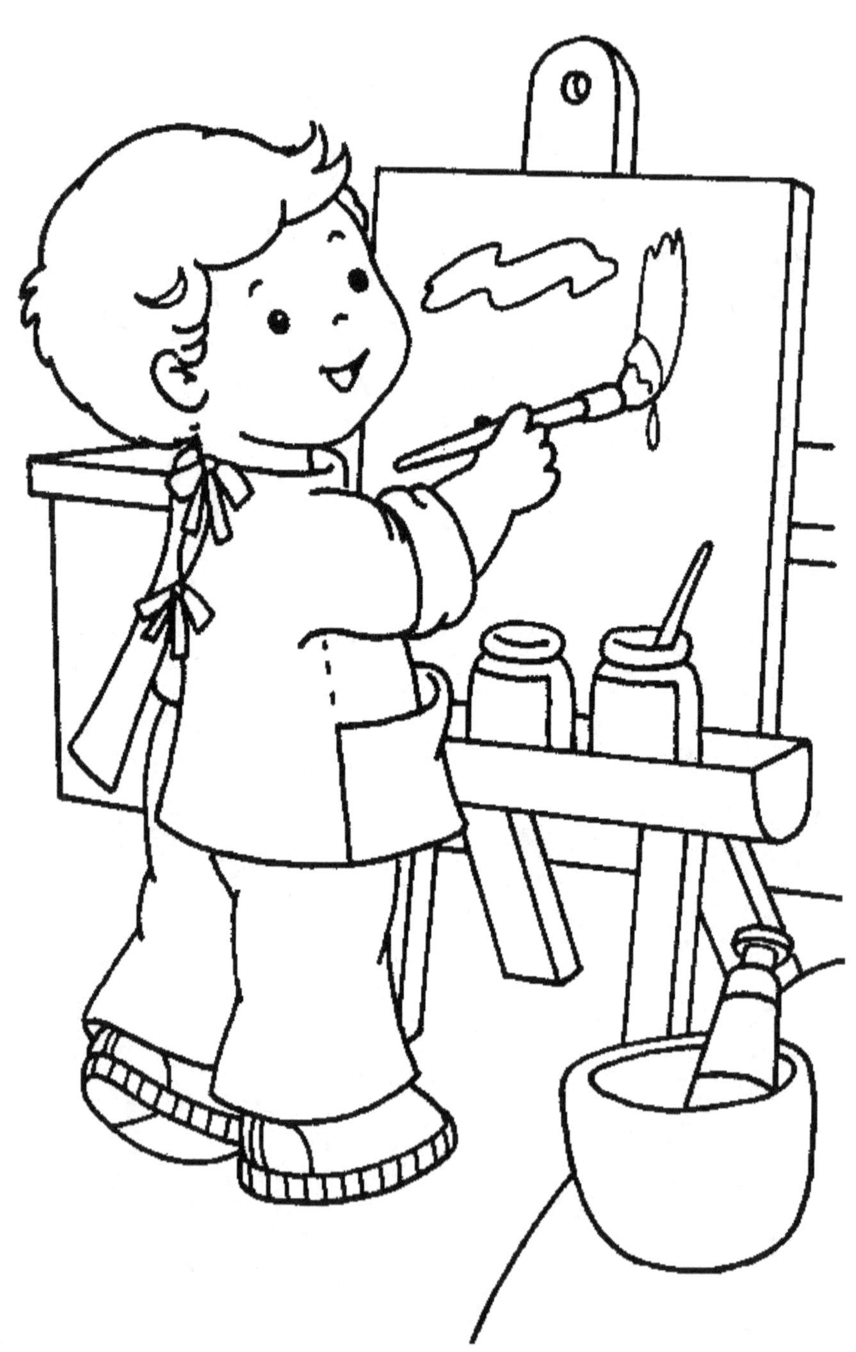

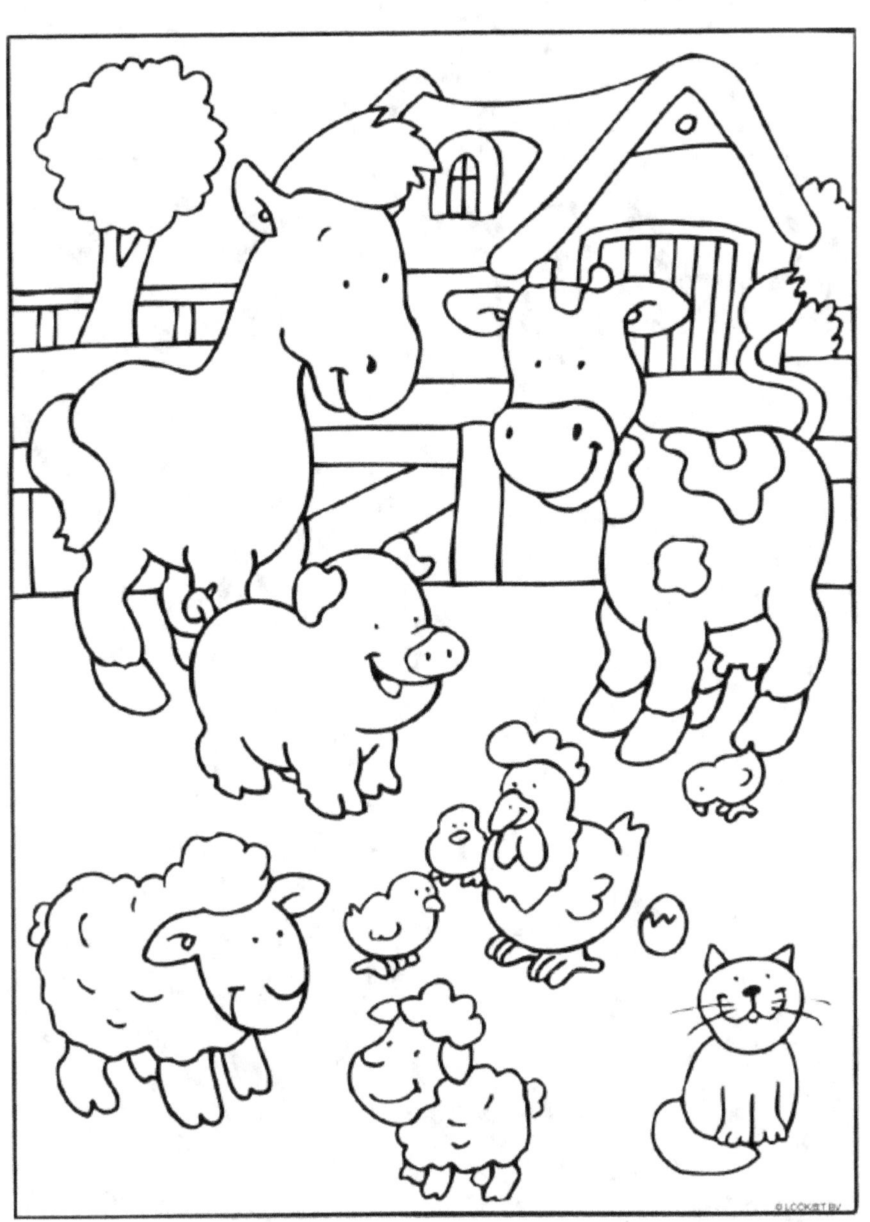

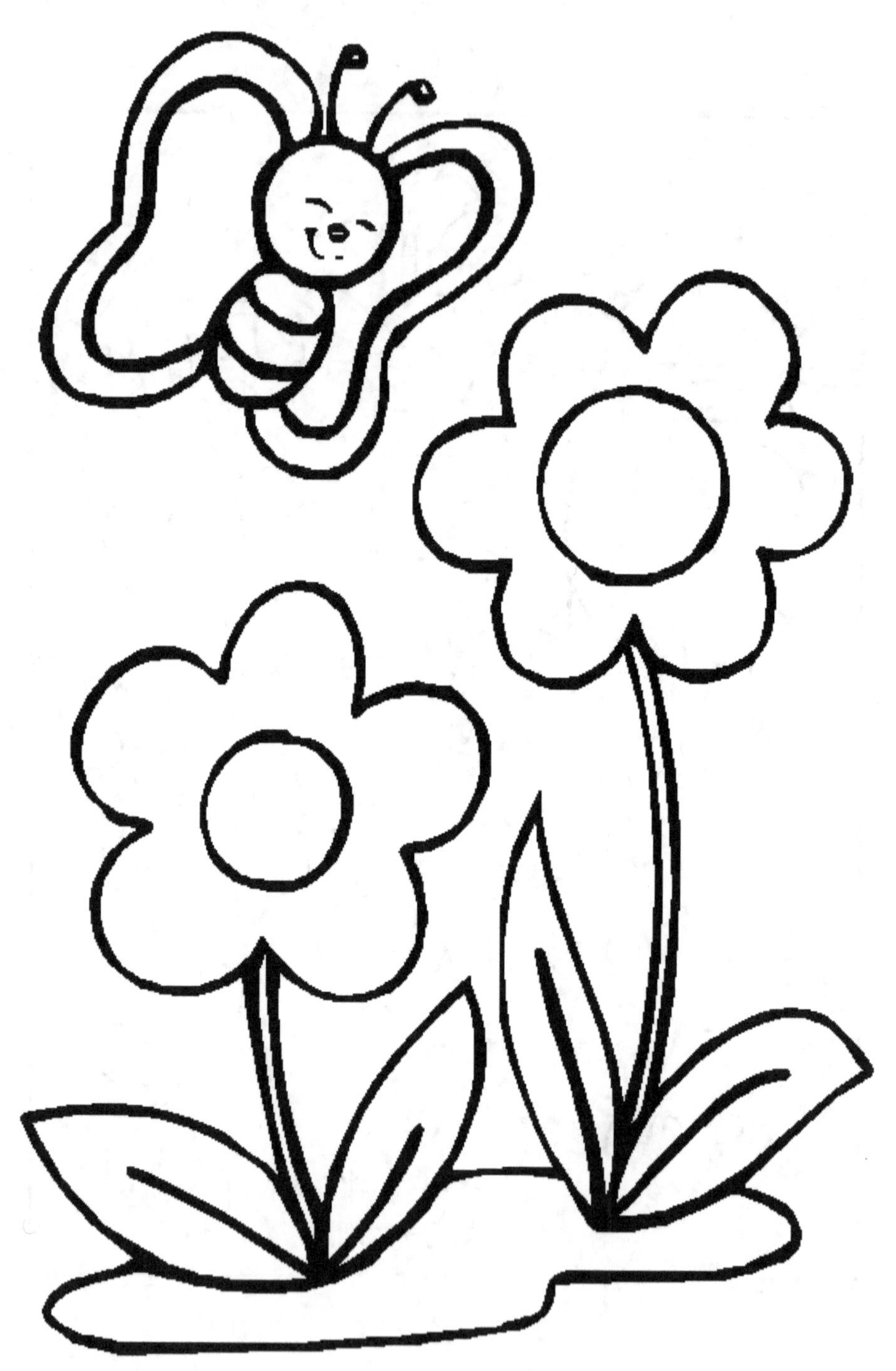

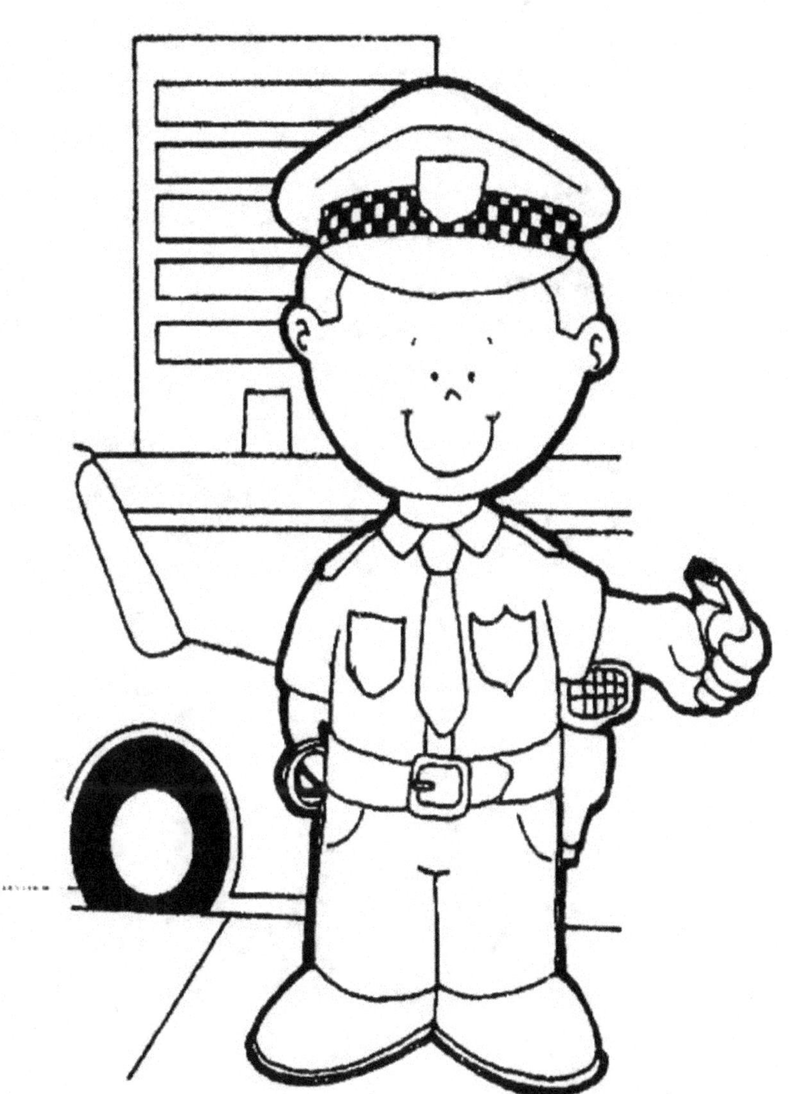

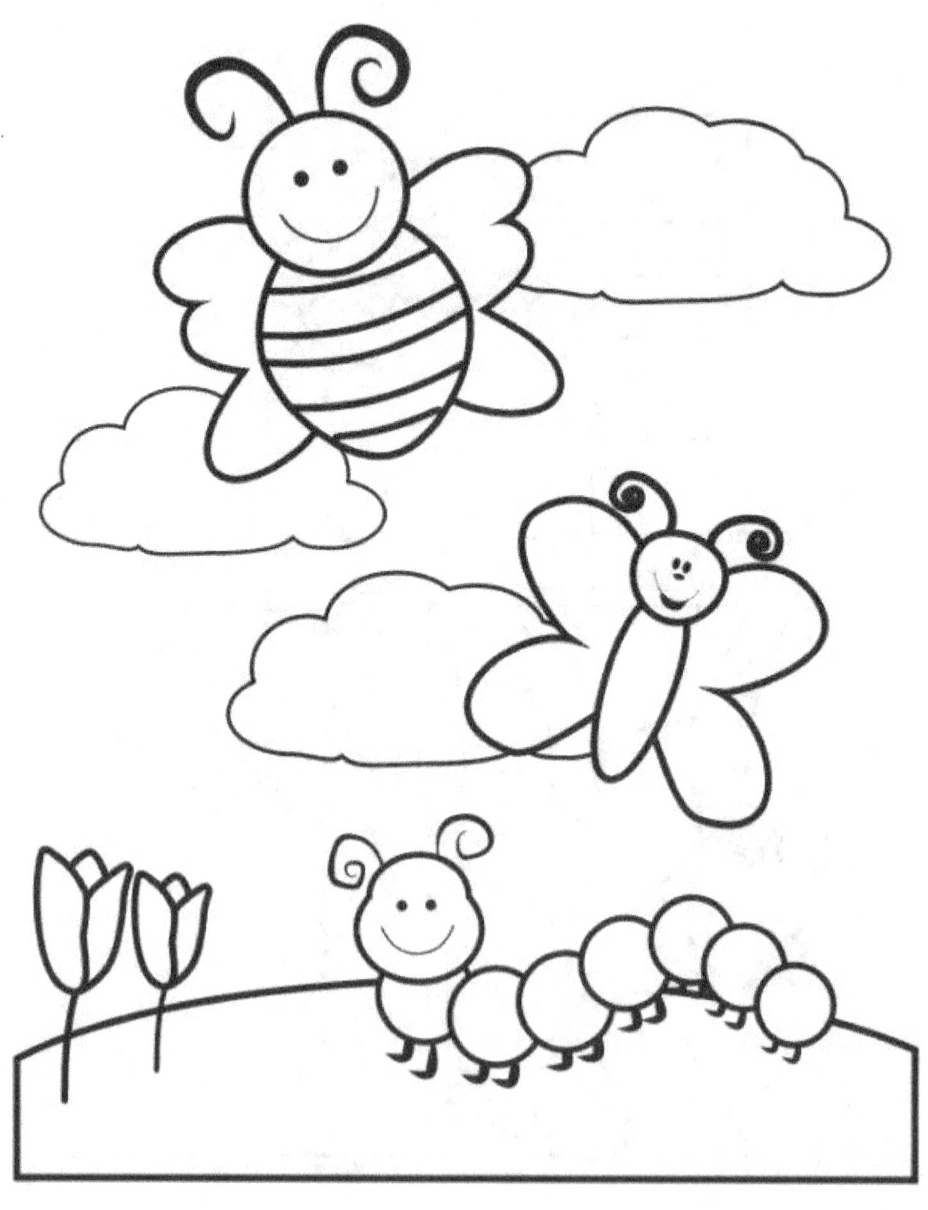

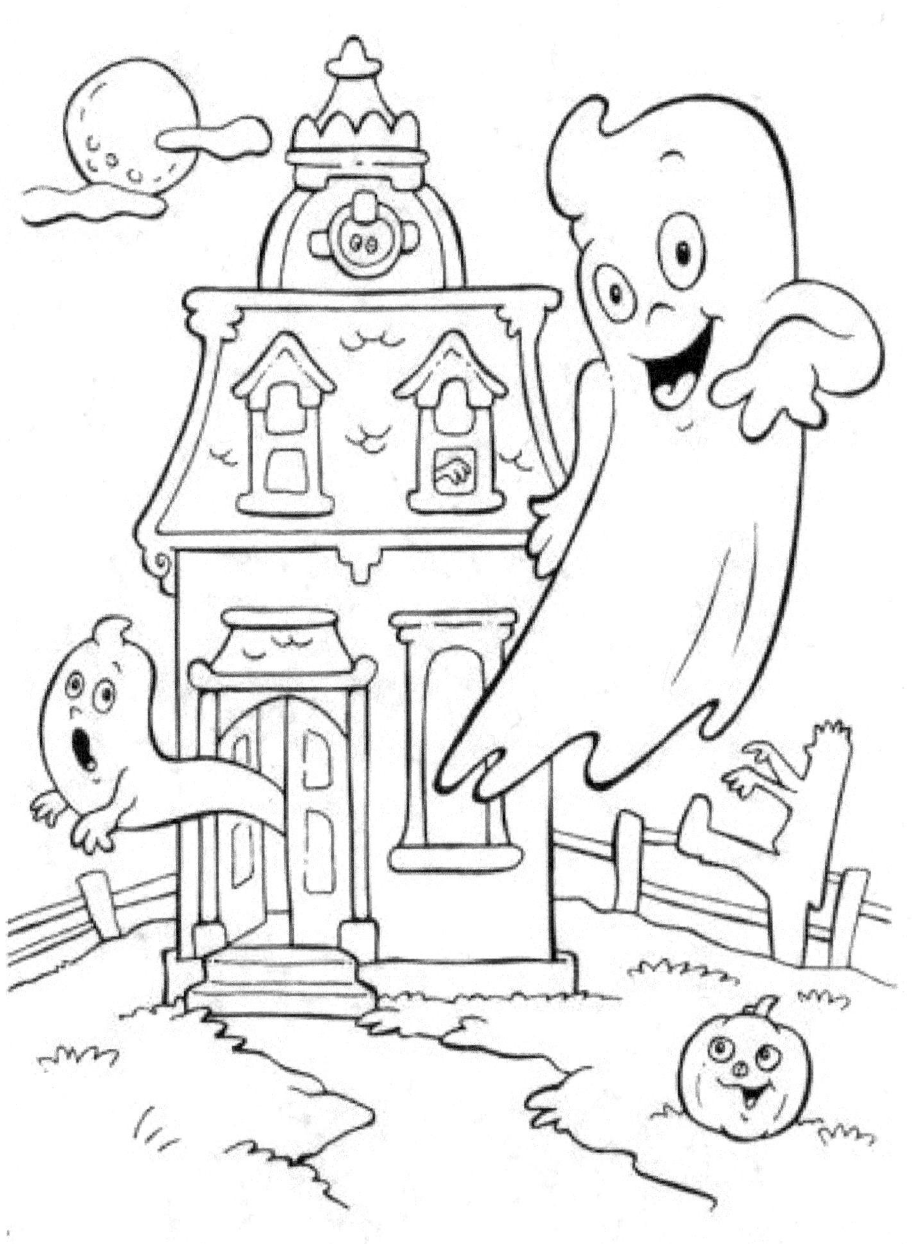

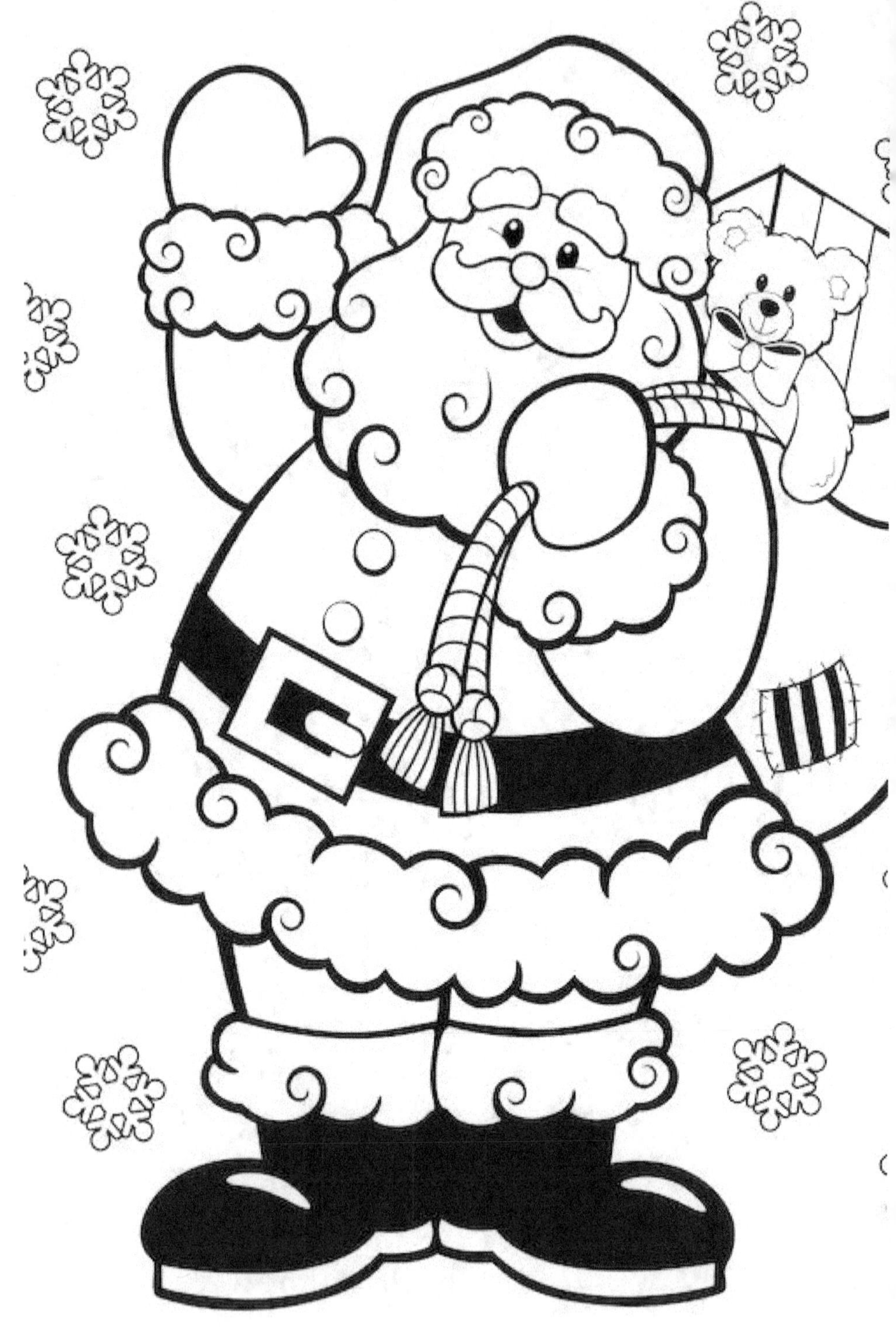

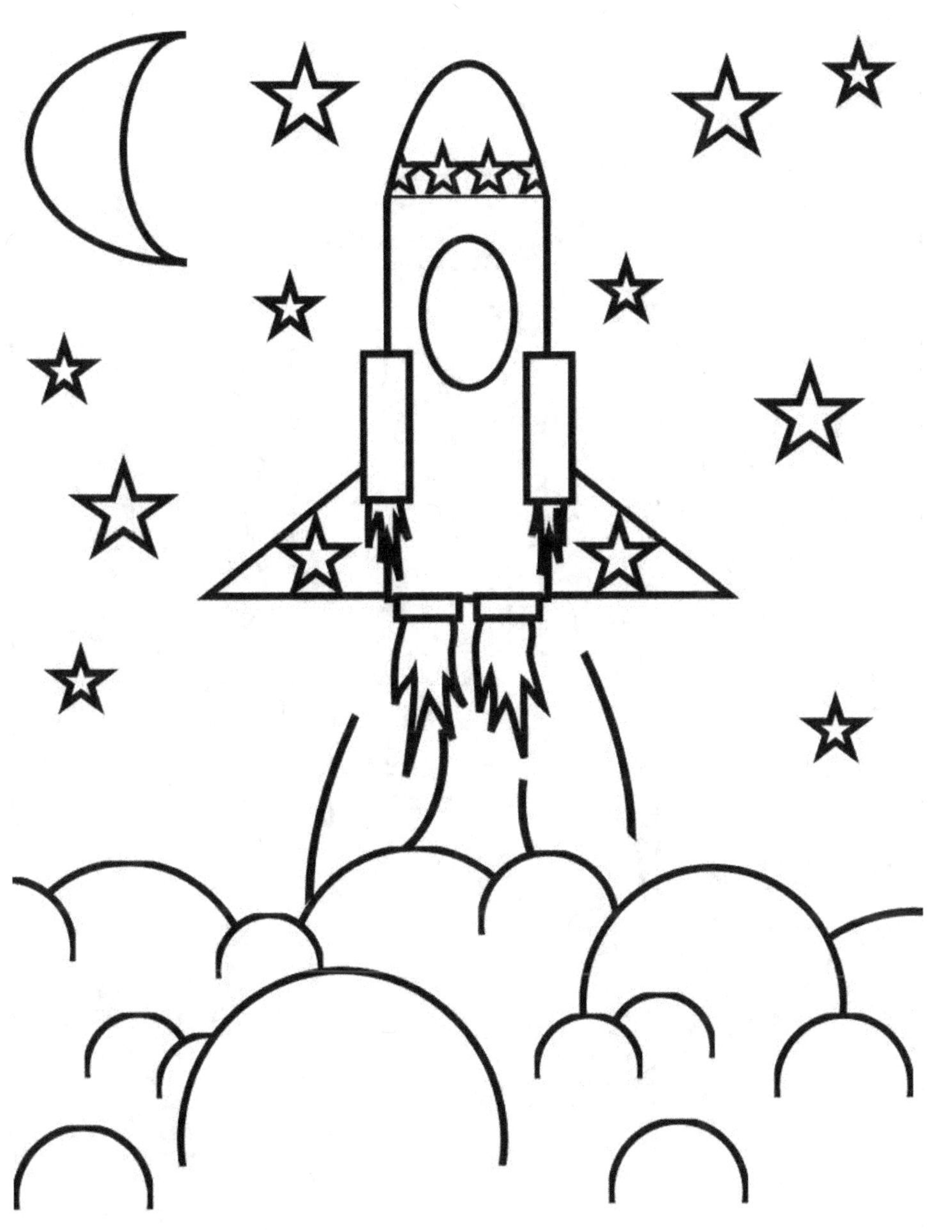

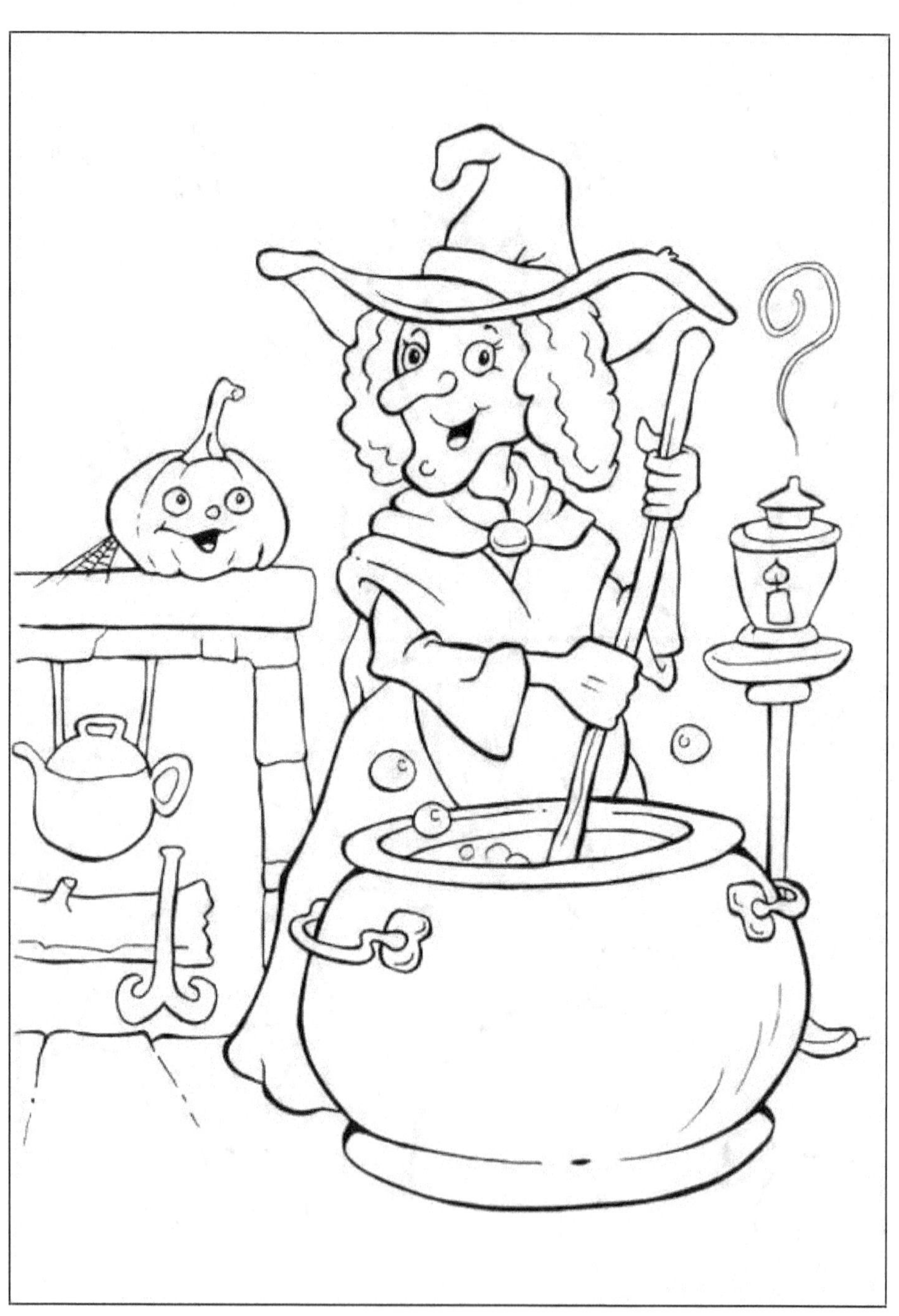

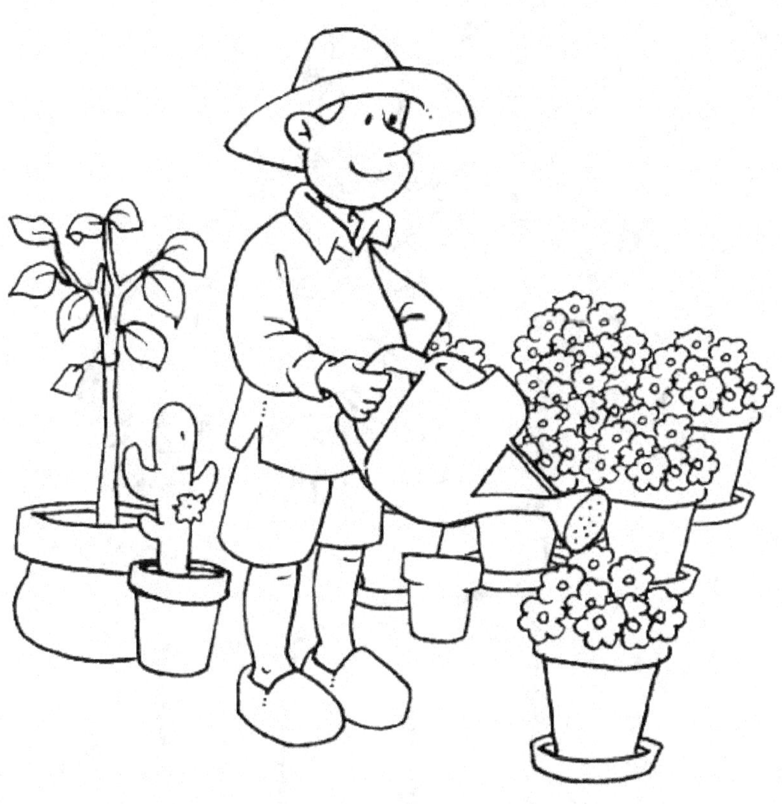

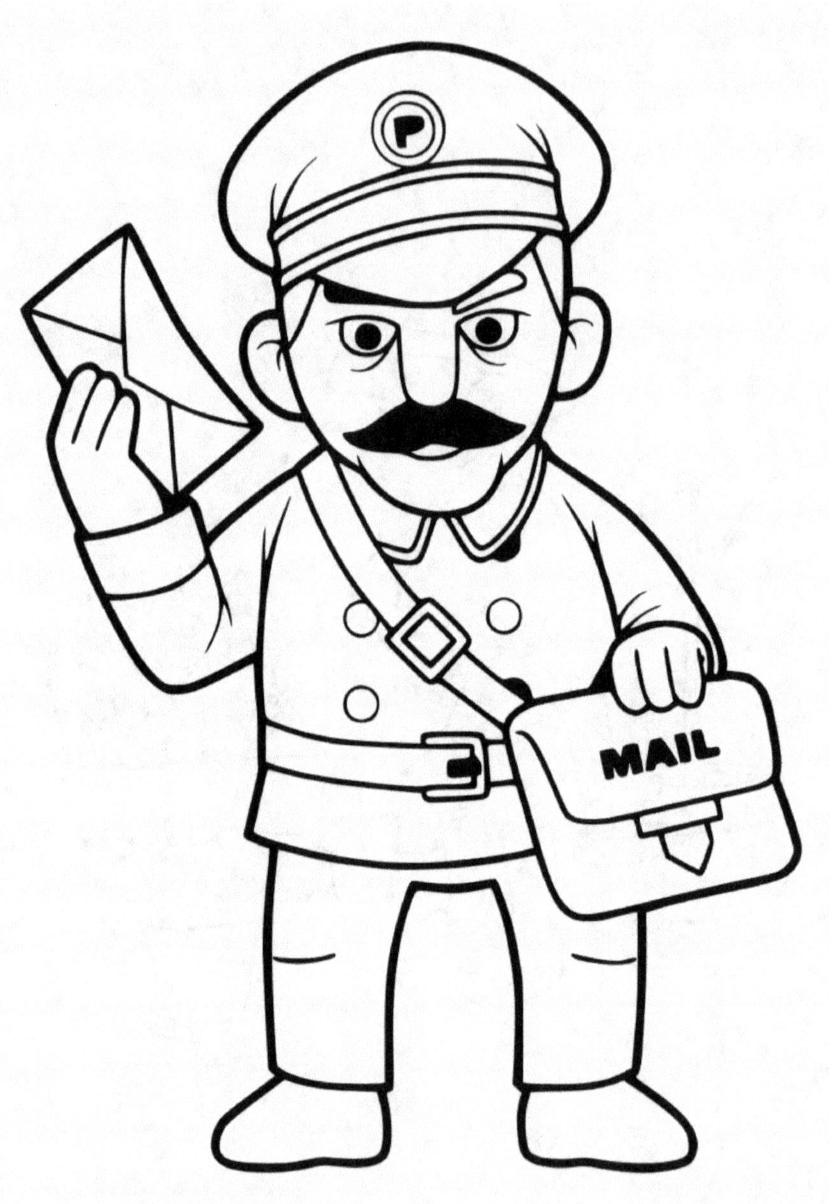

MAIL

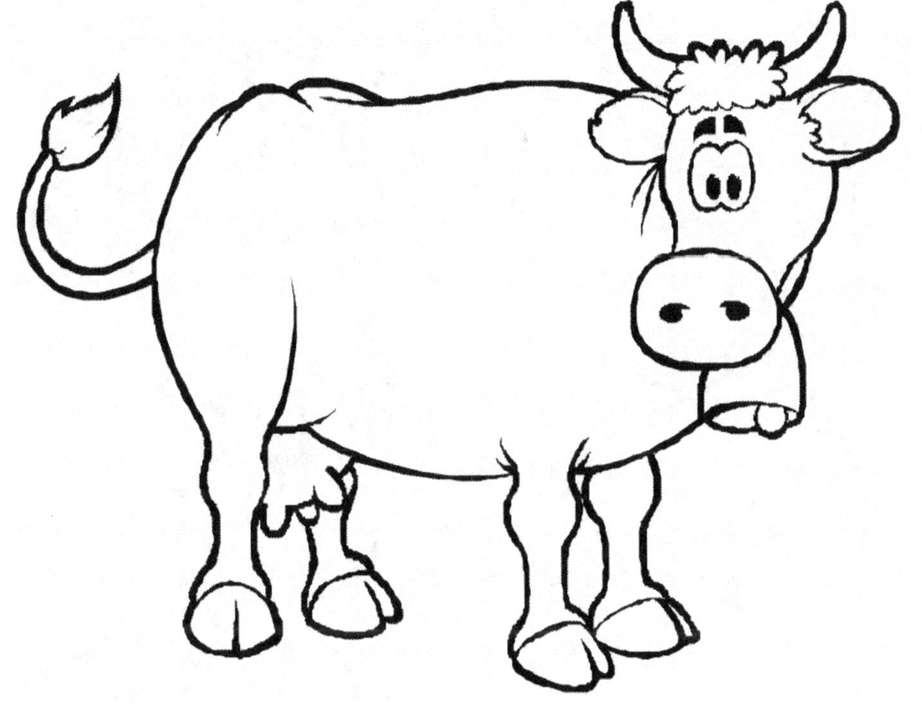

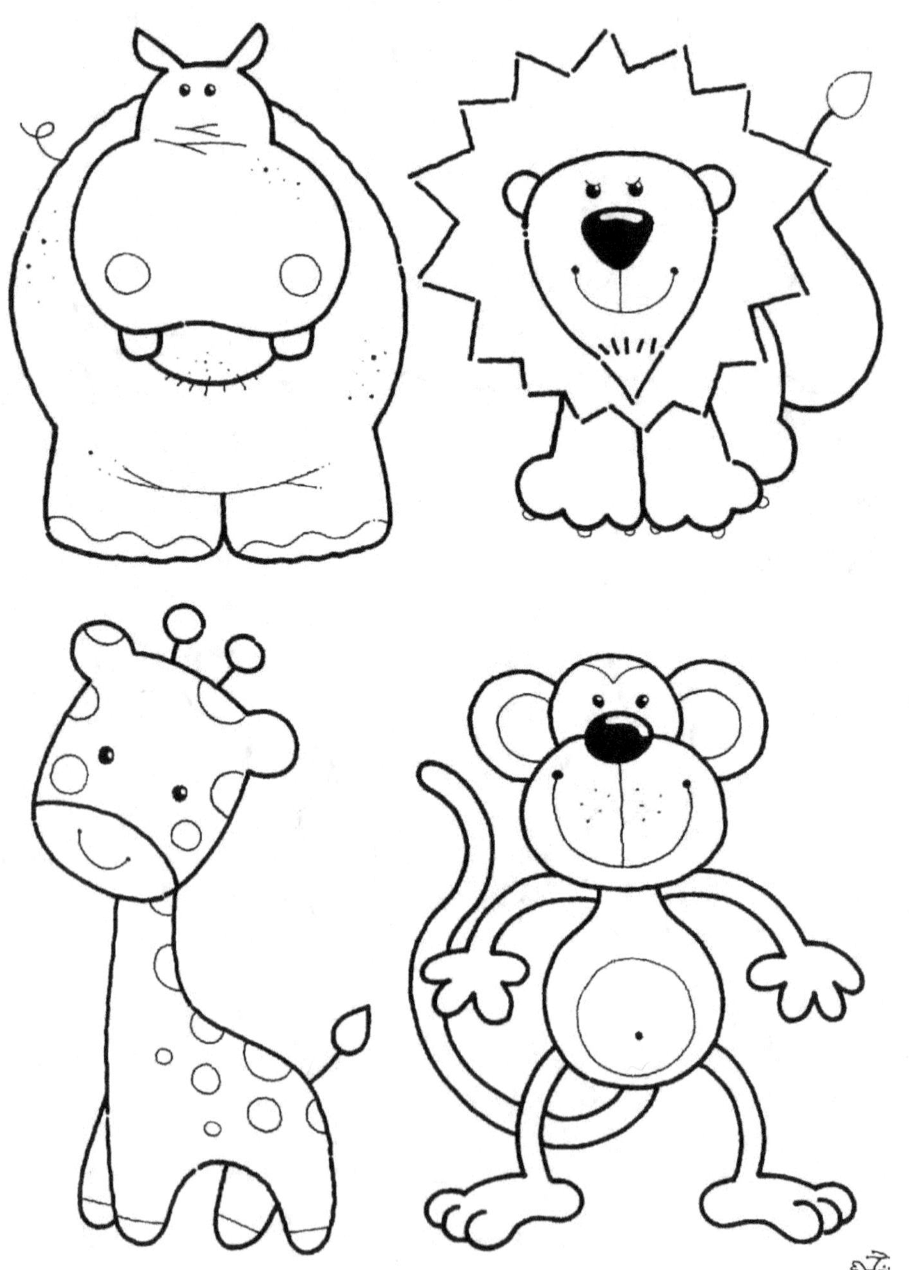

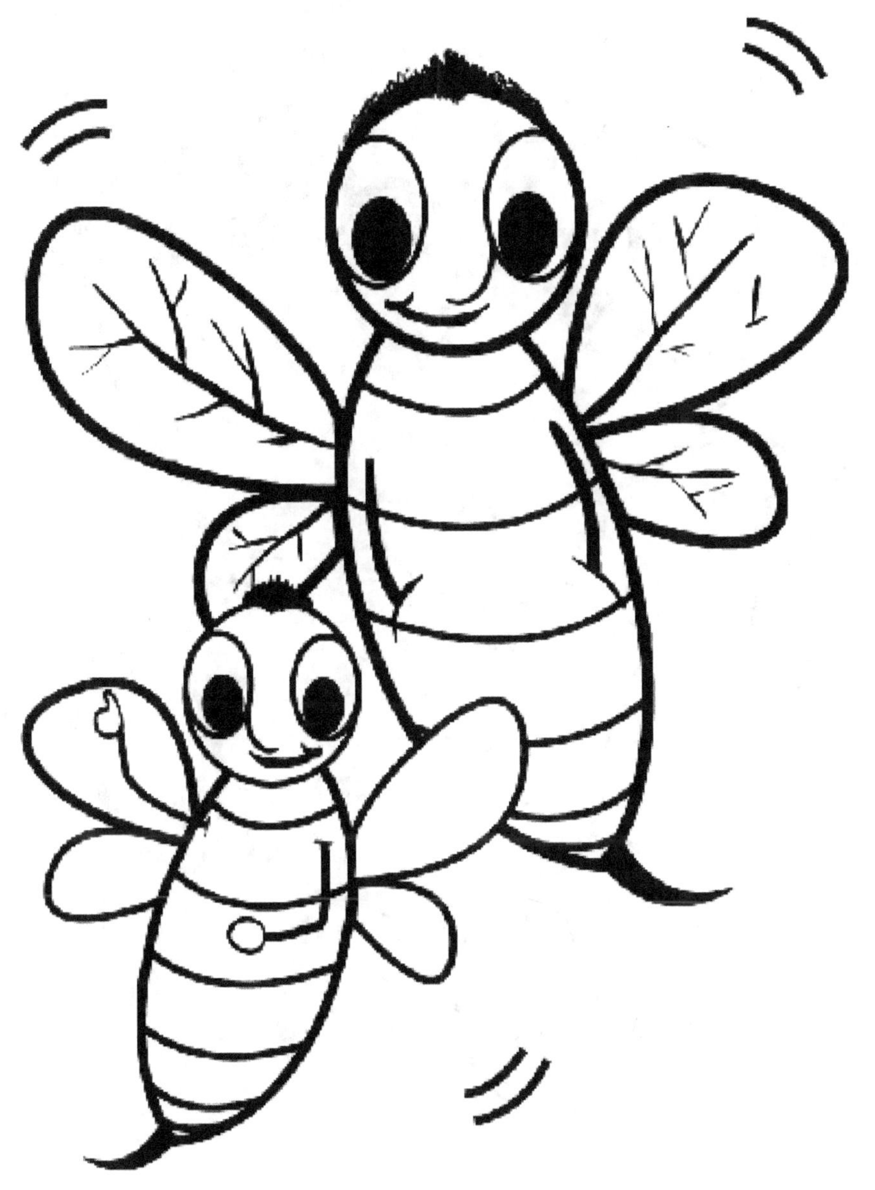

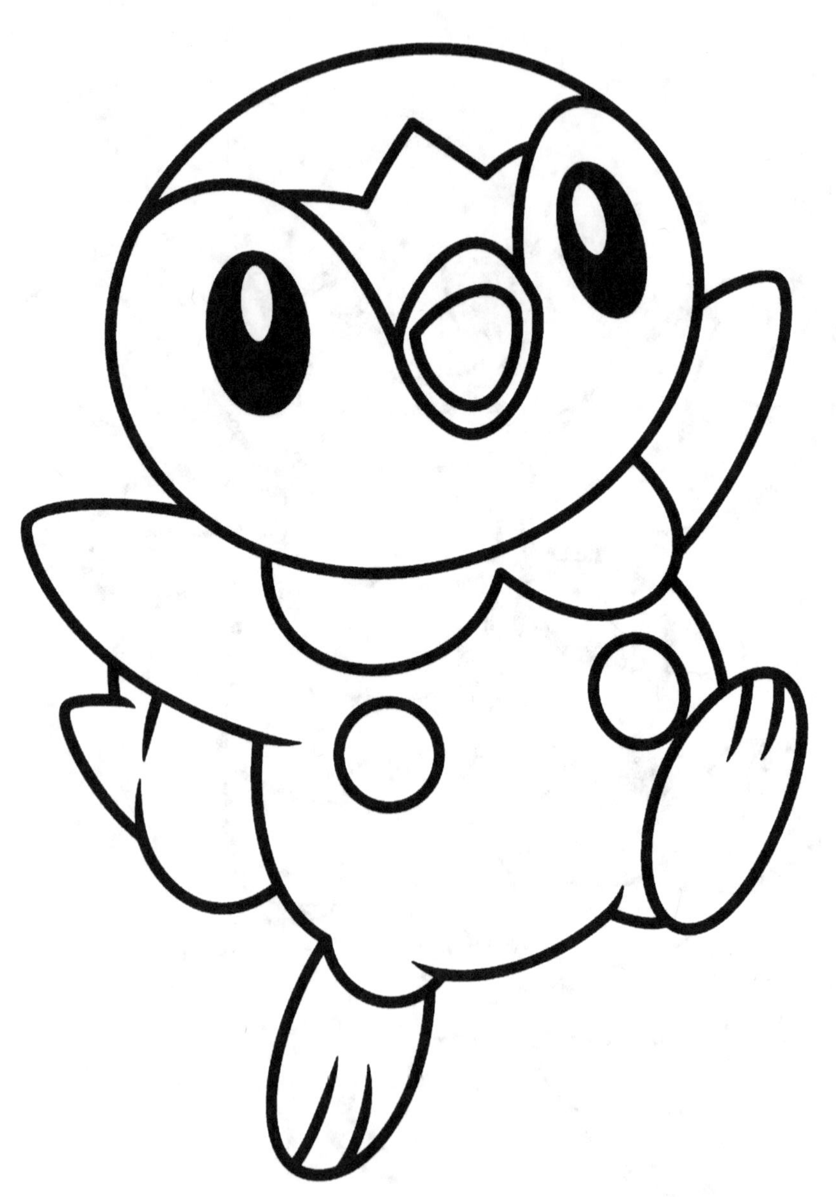

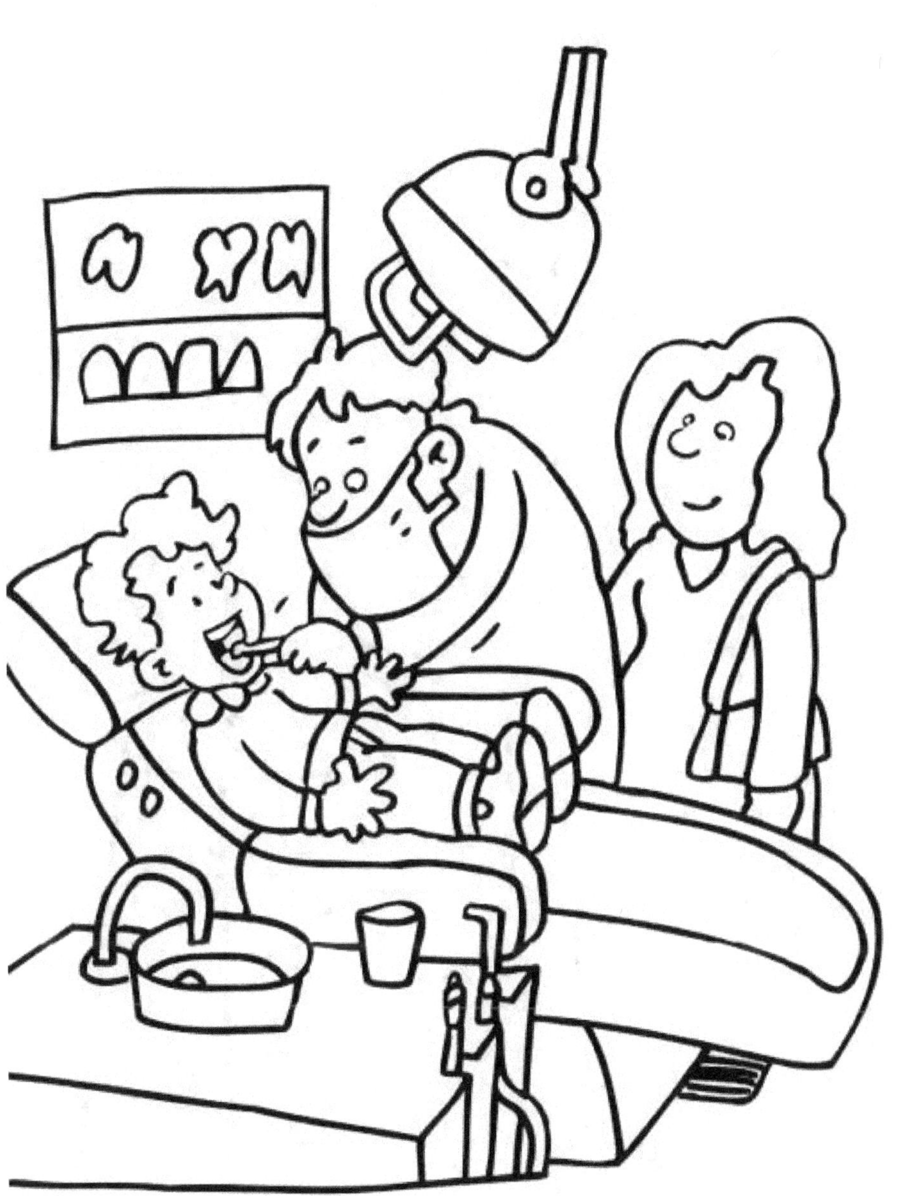

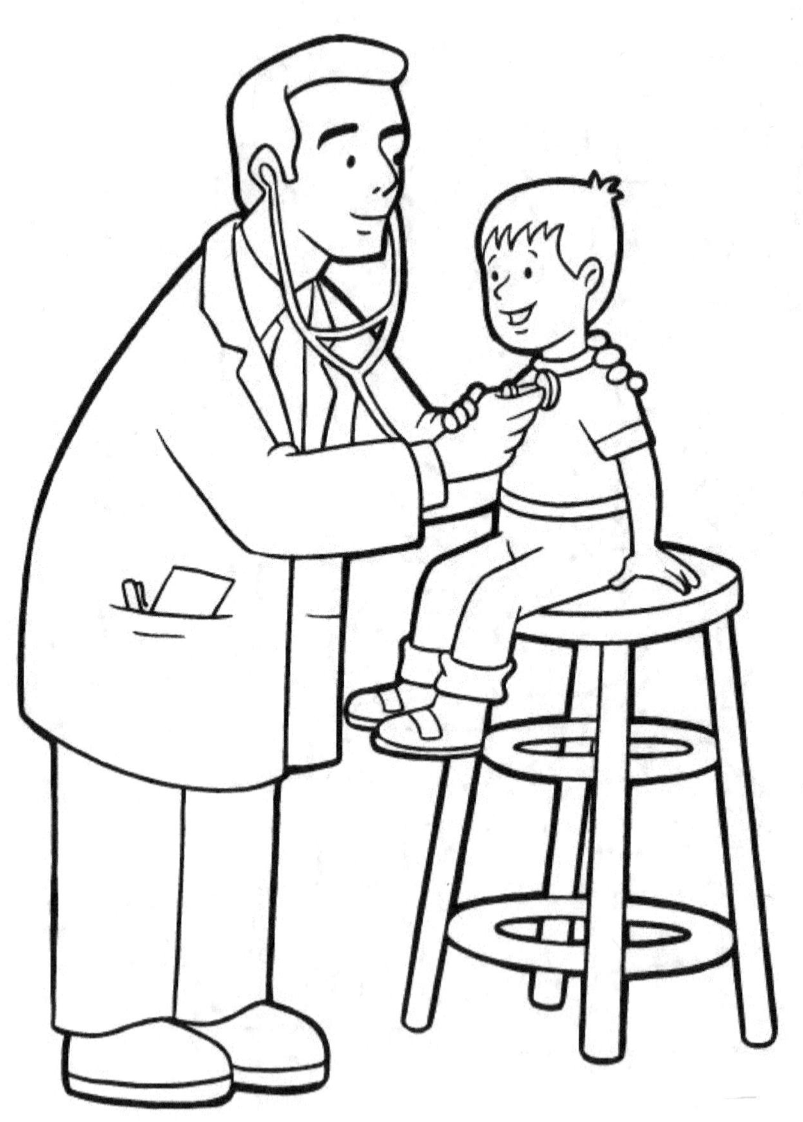

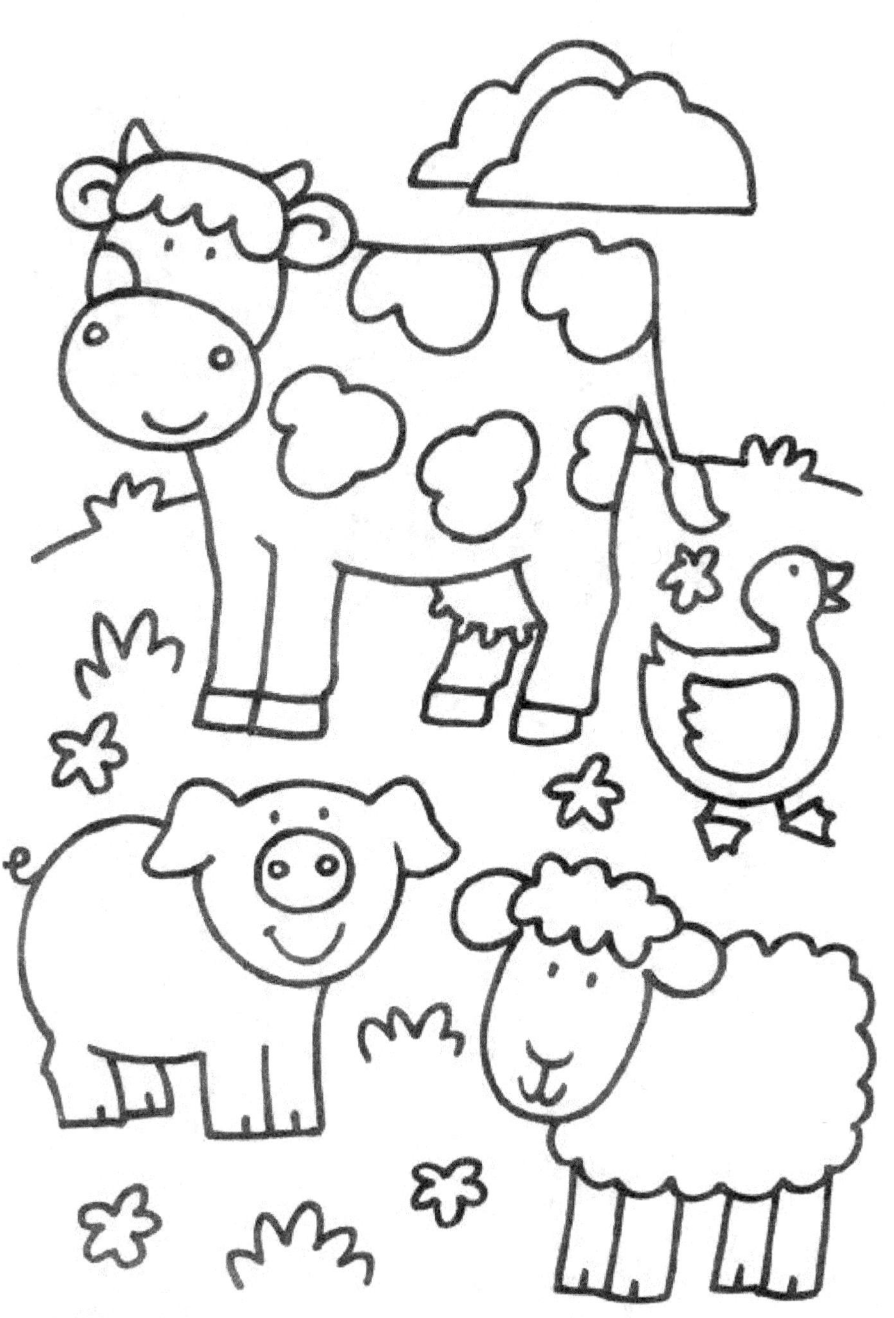

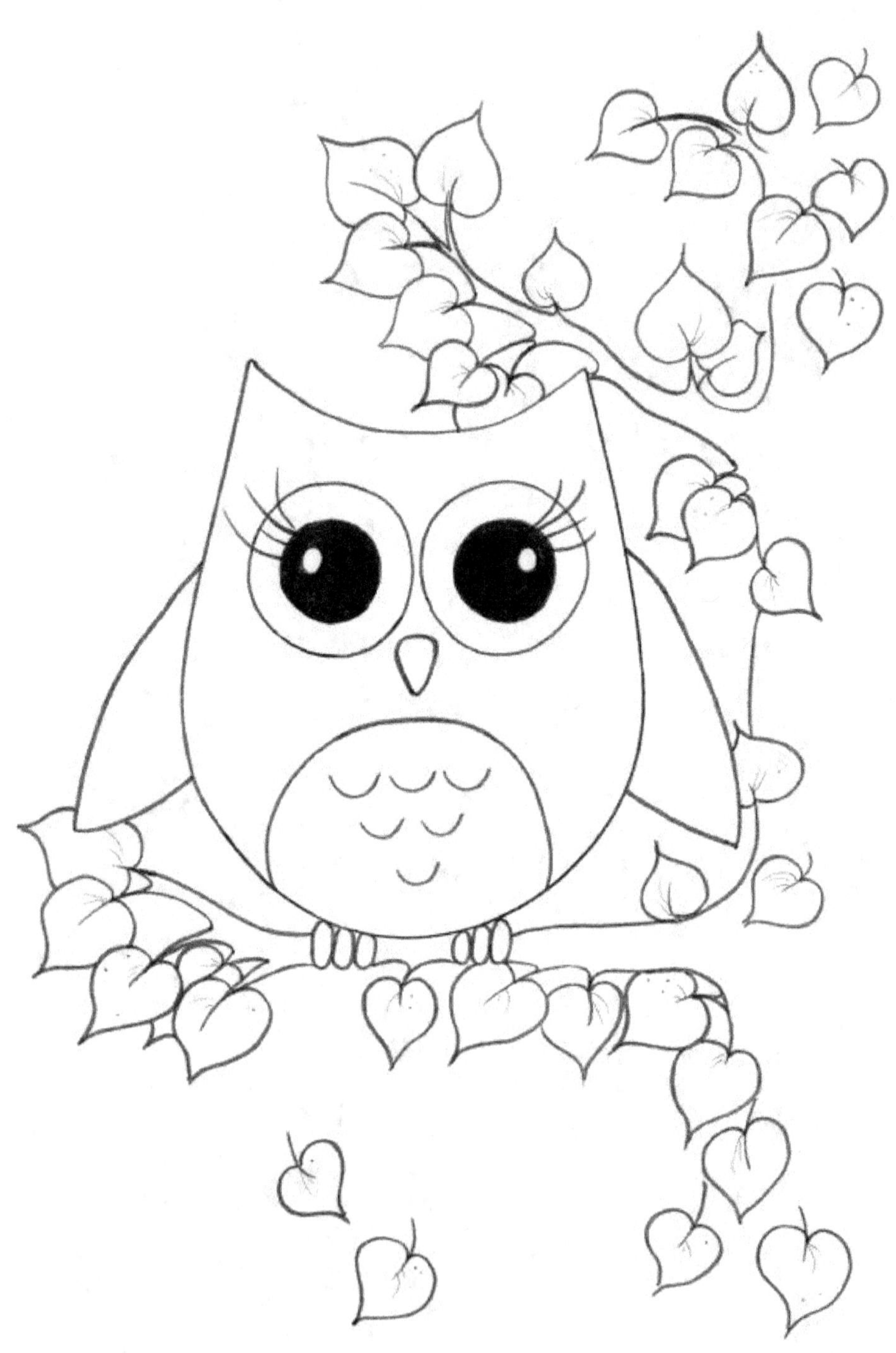

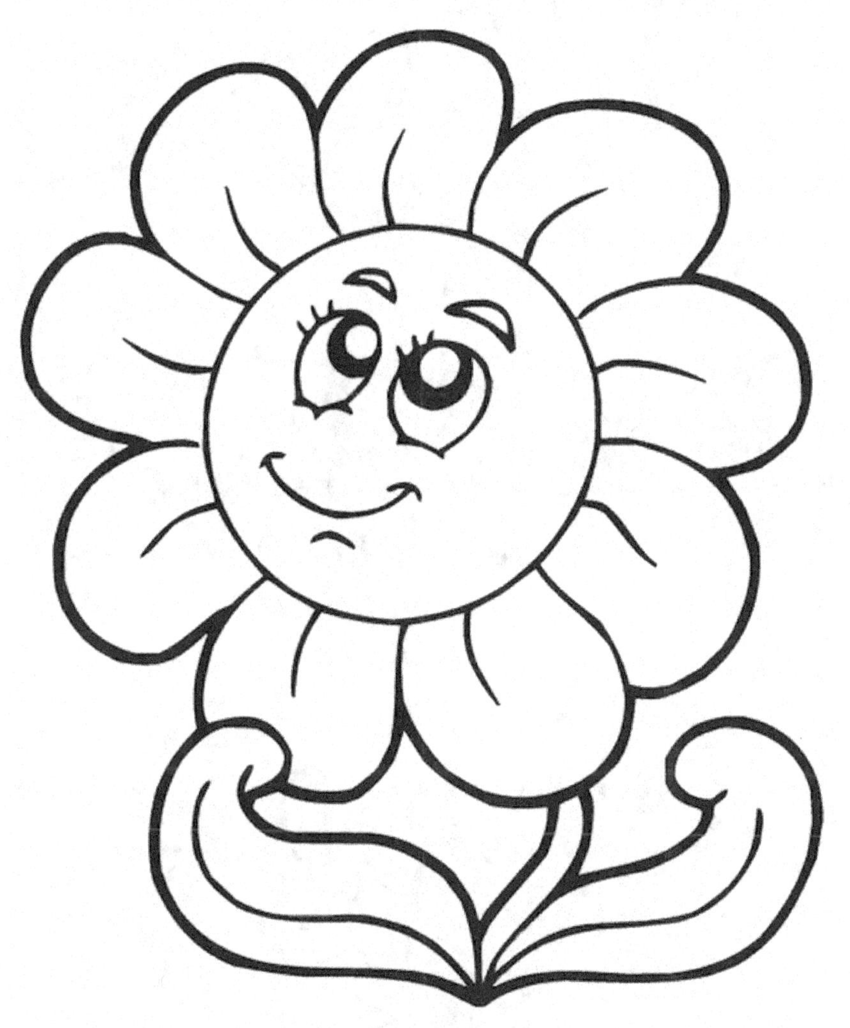

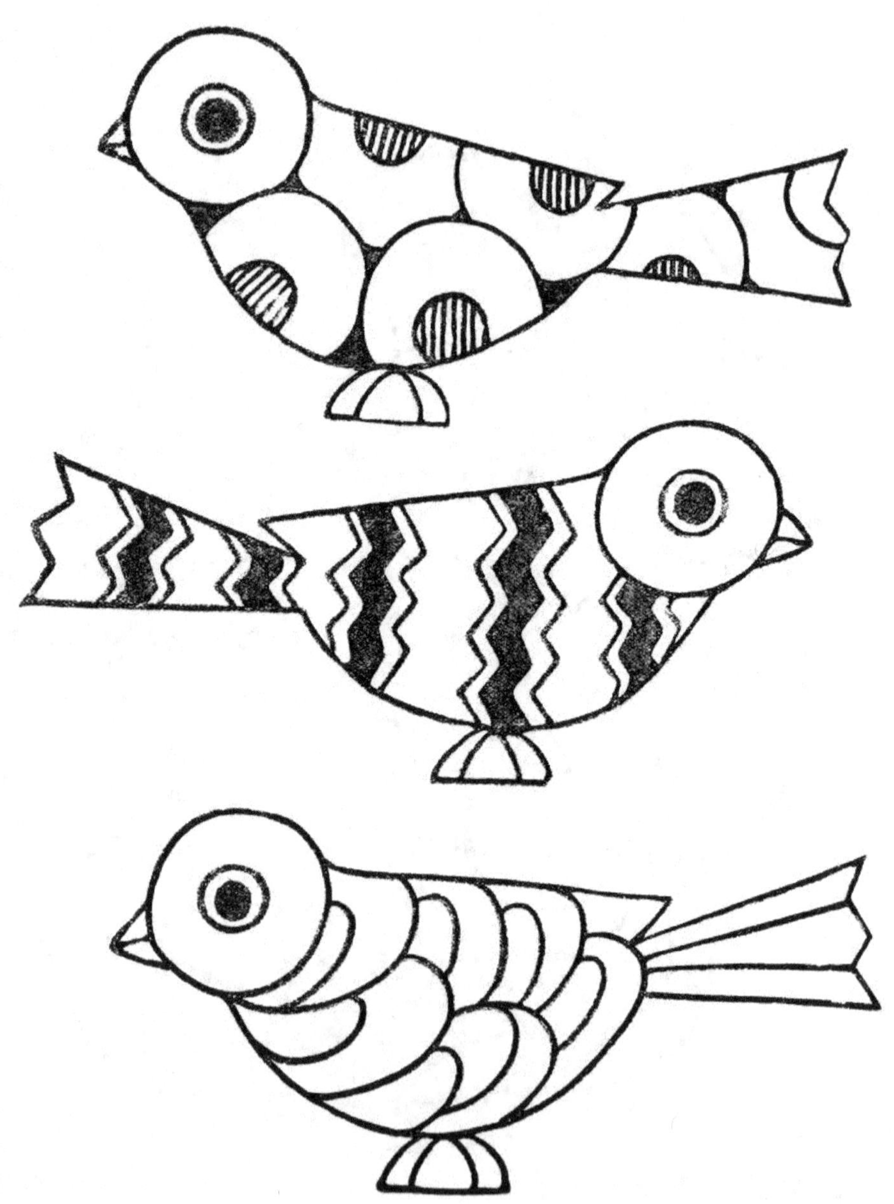

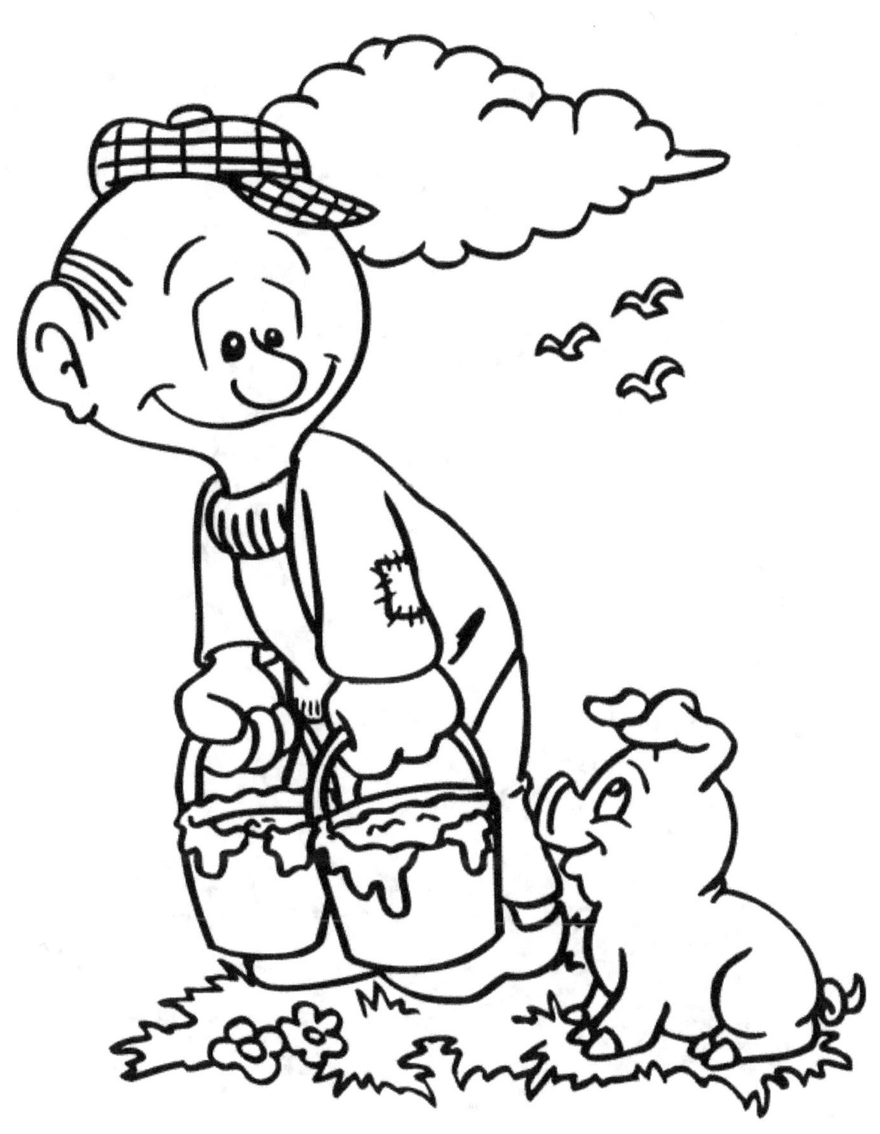

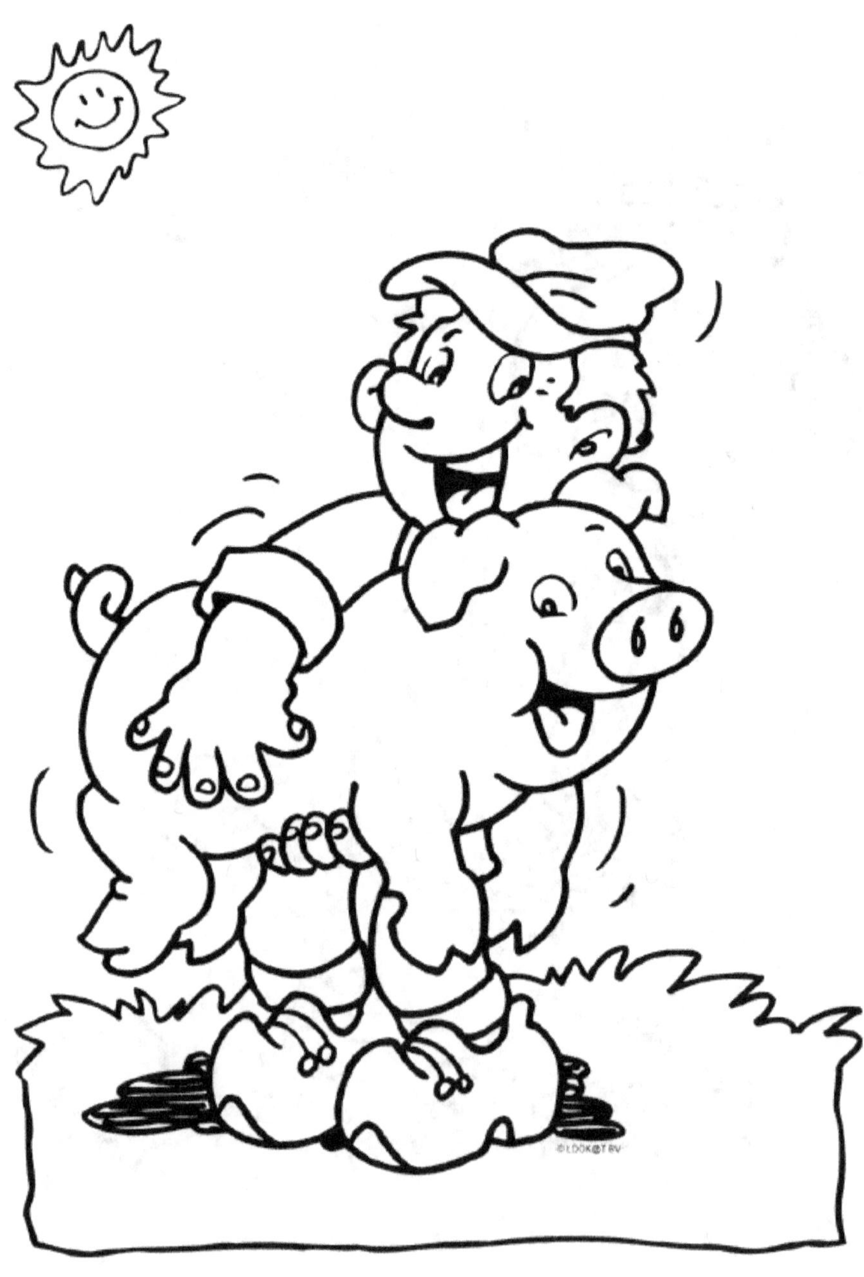

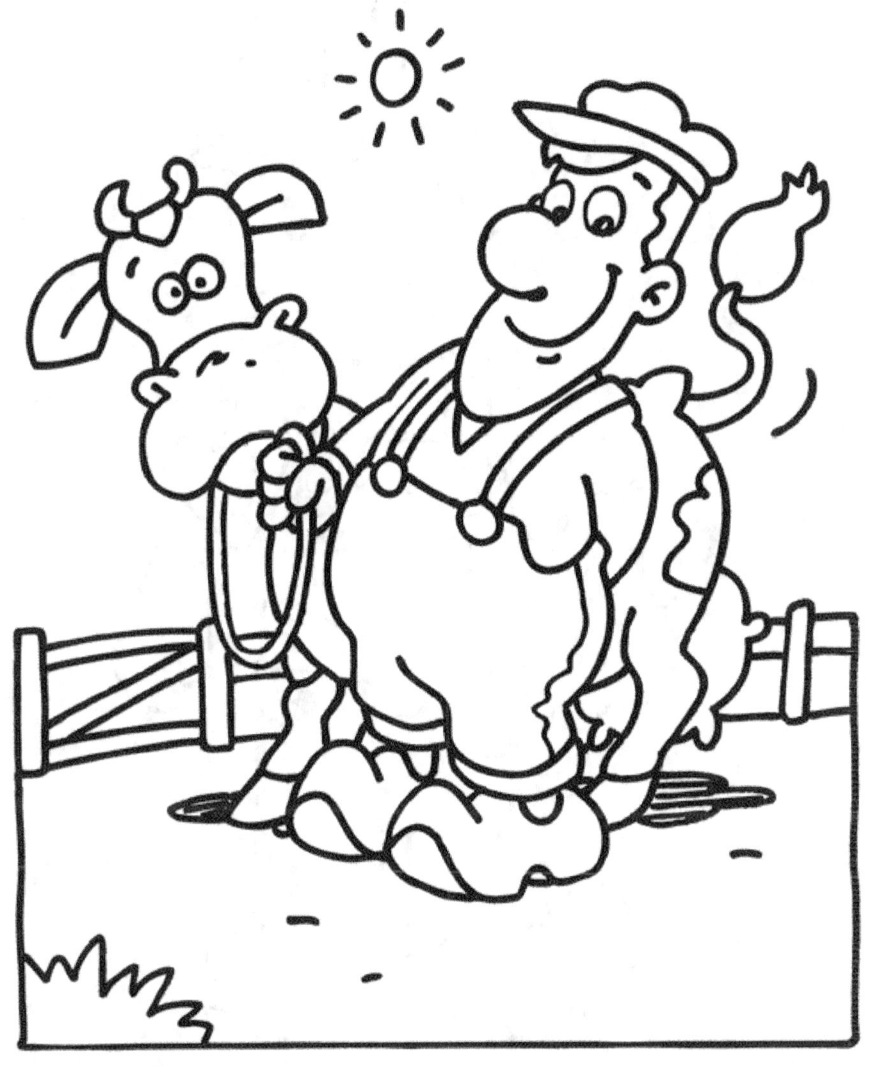

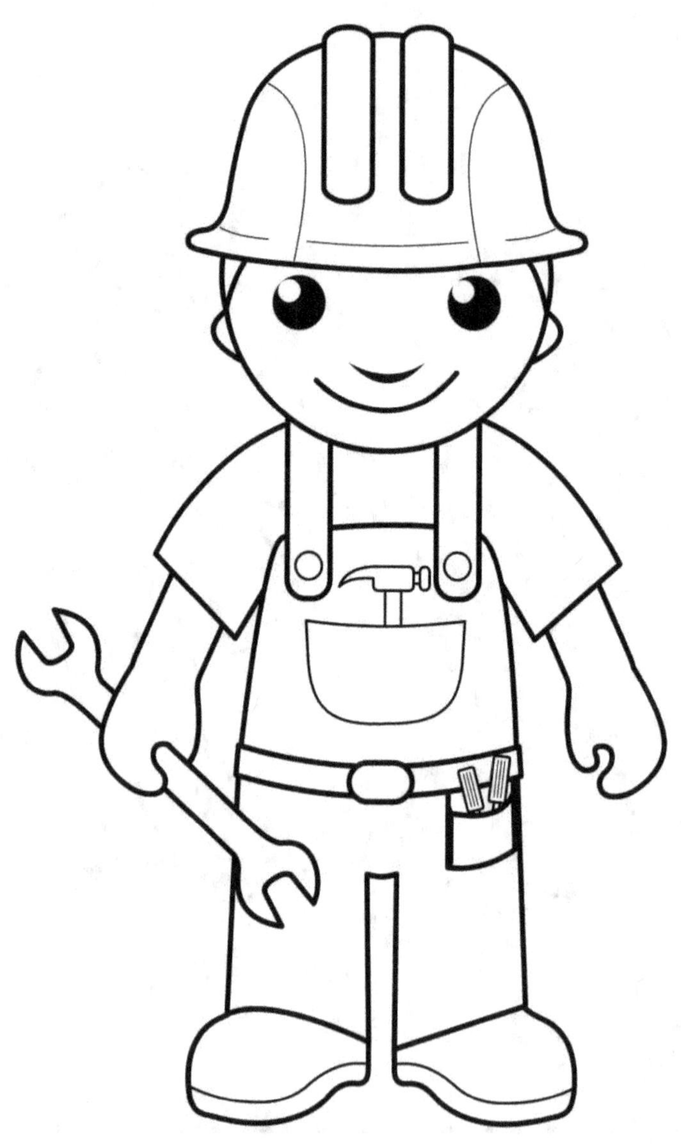

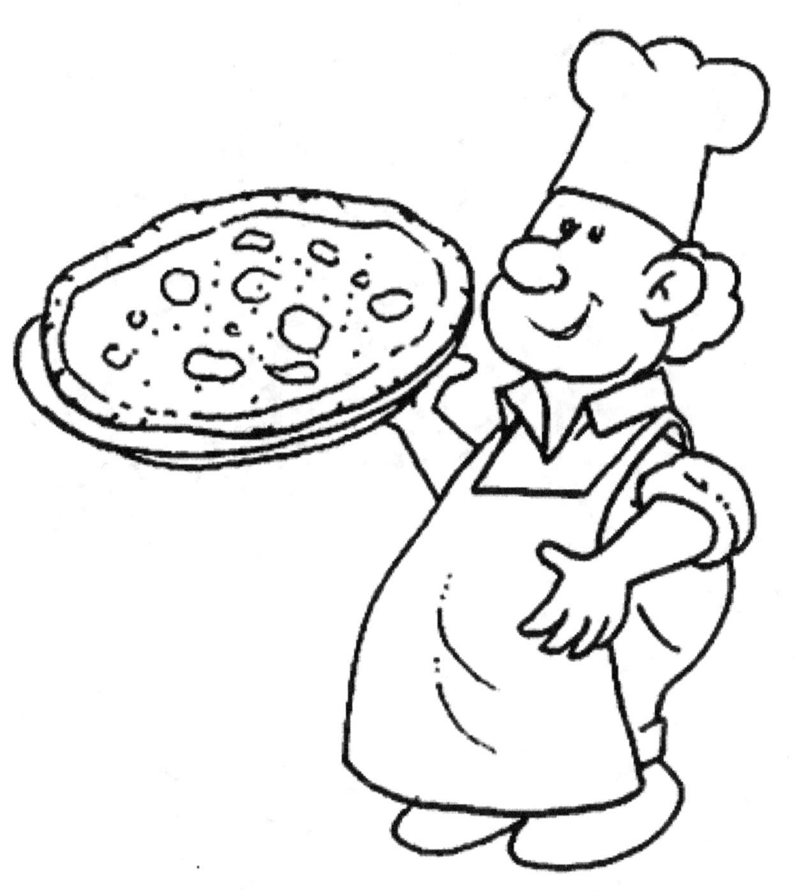

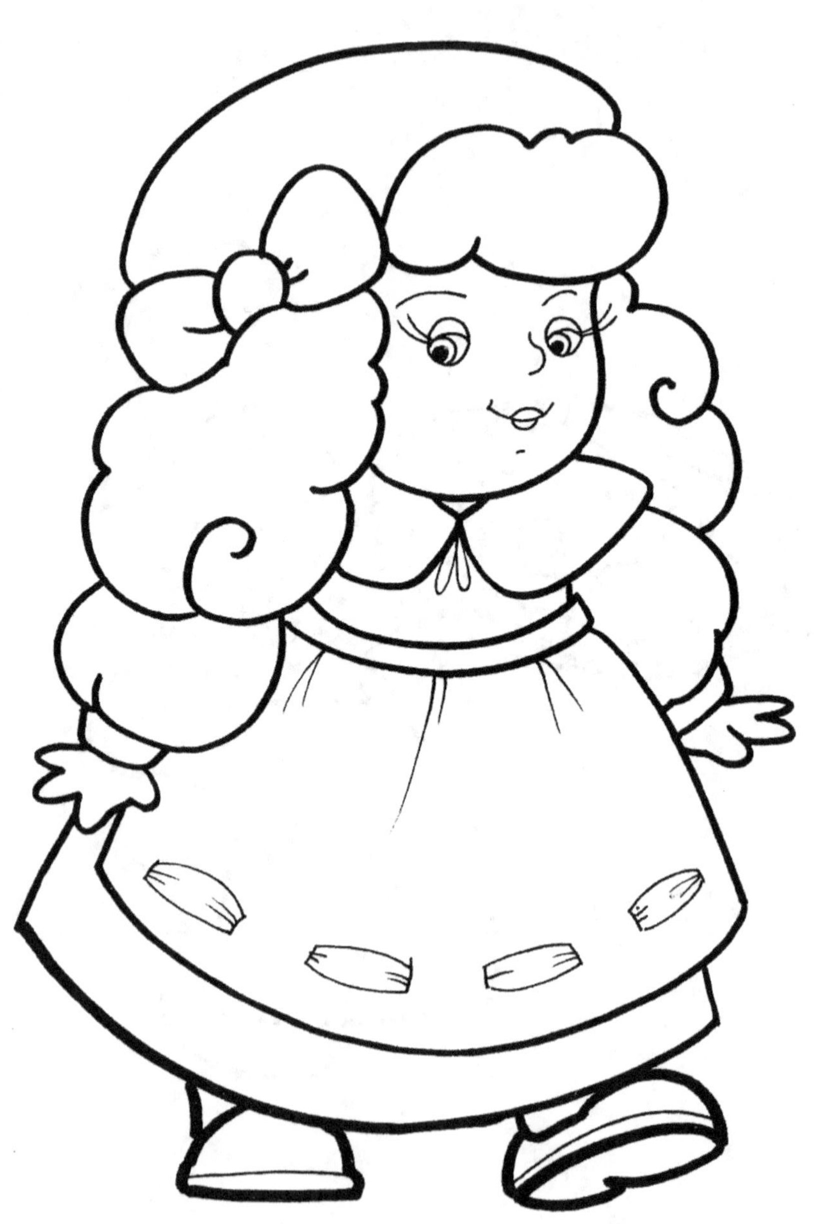

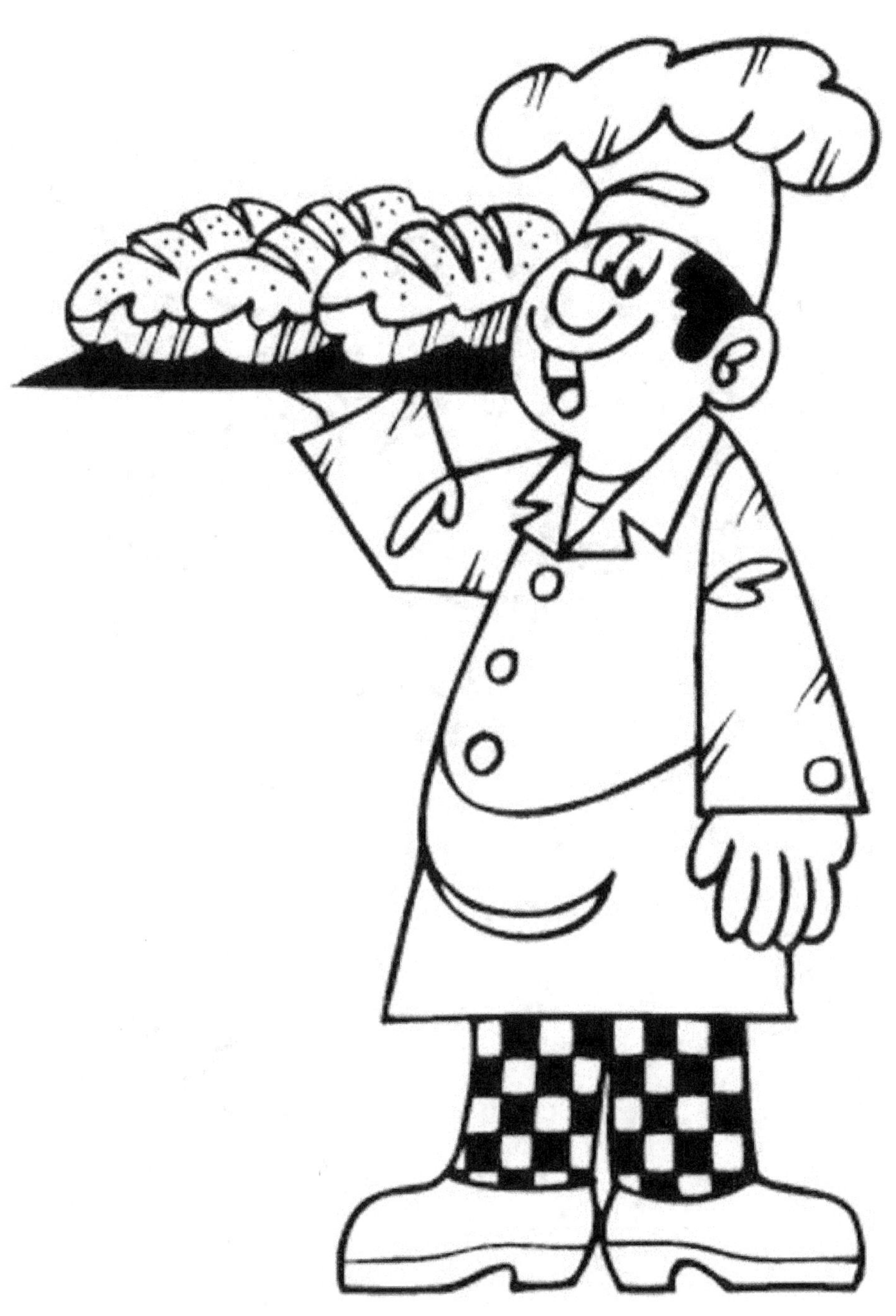

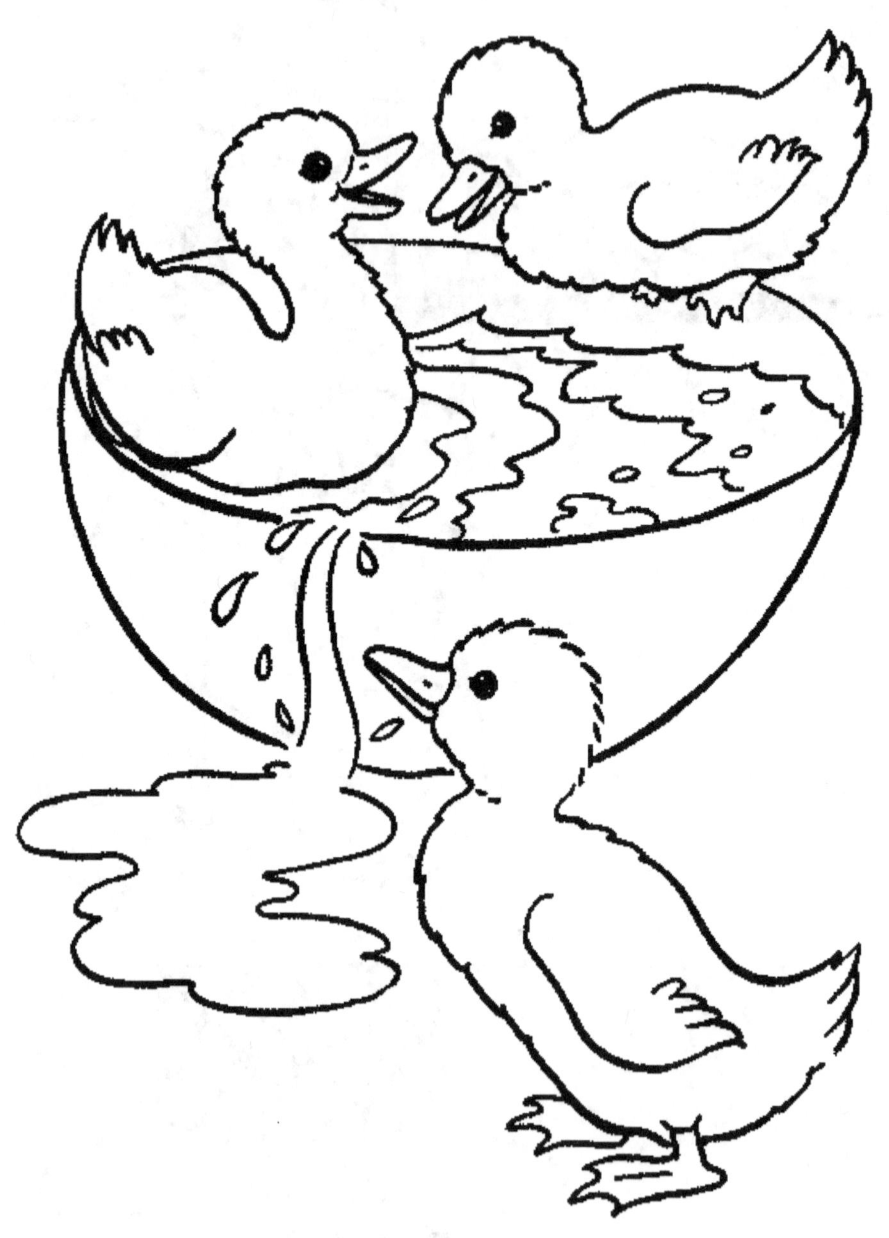

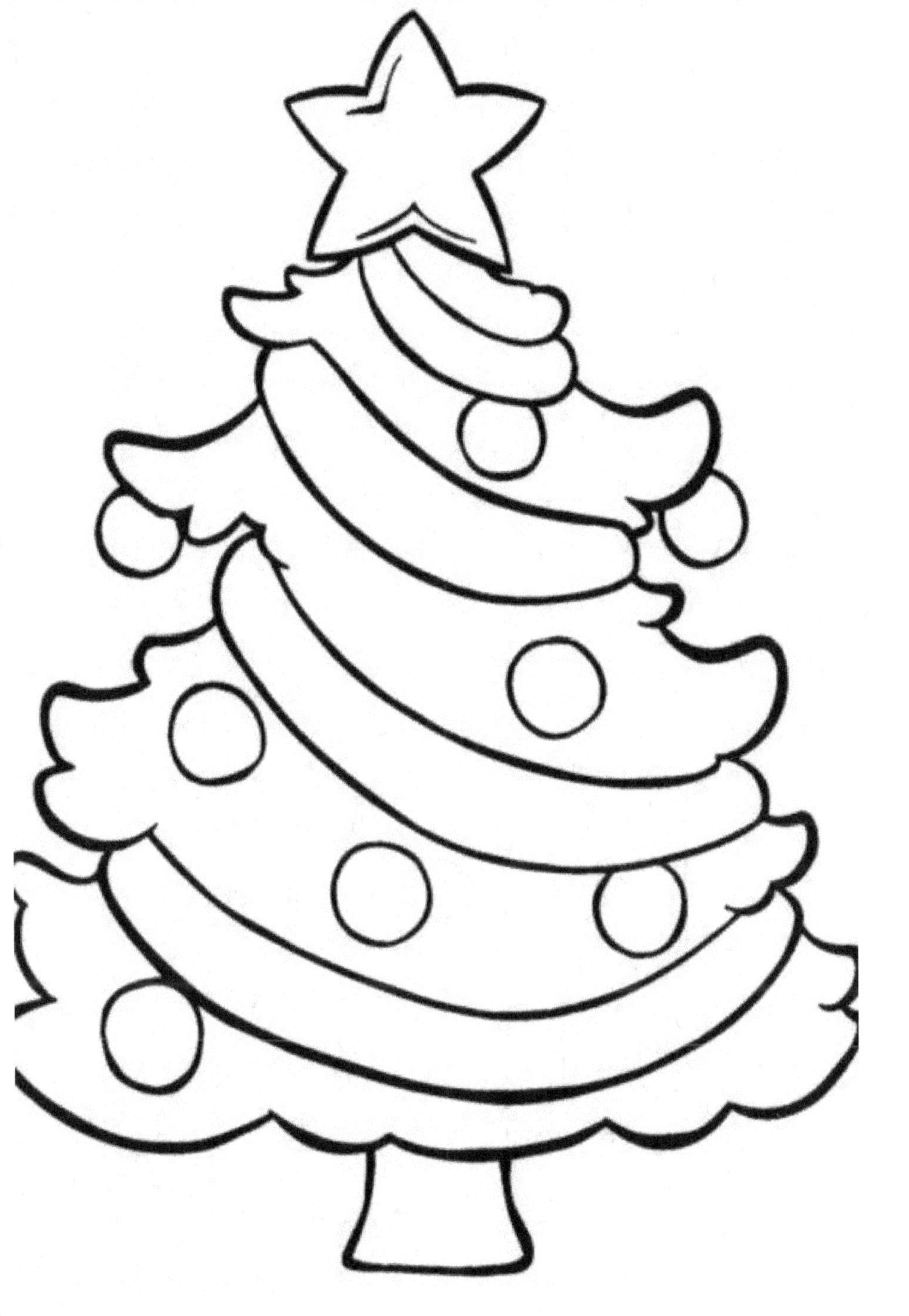

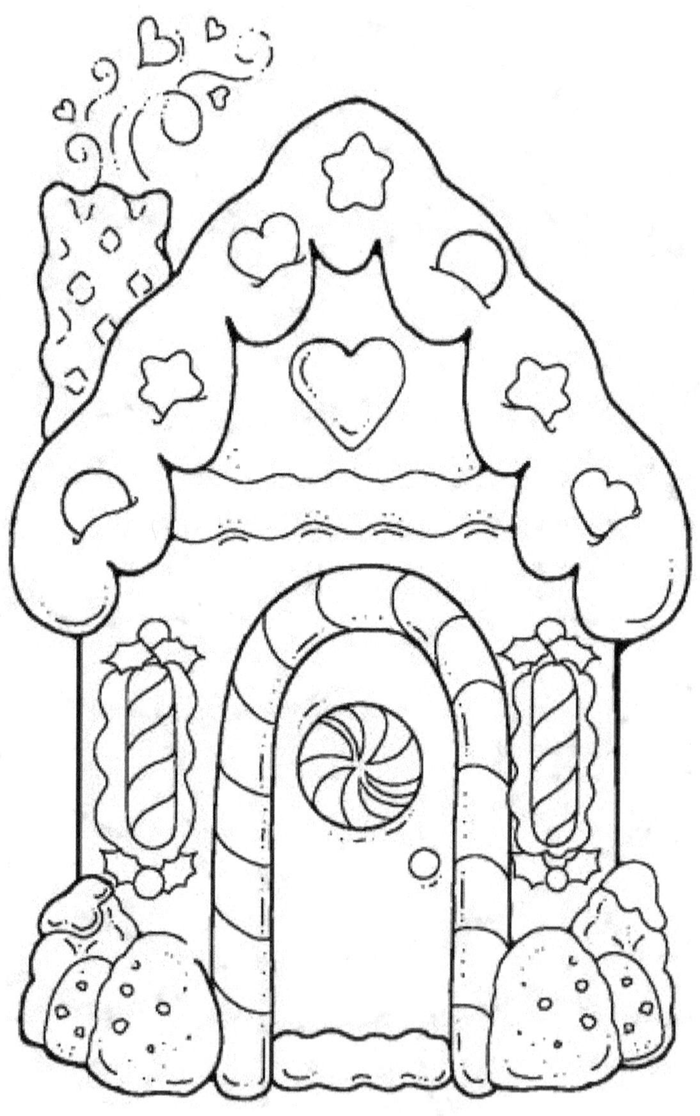

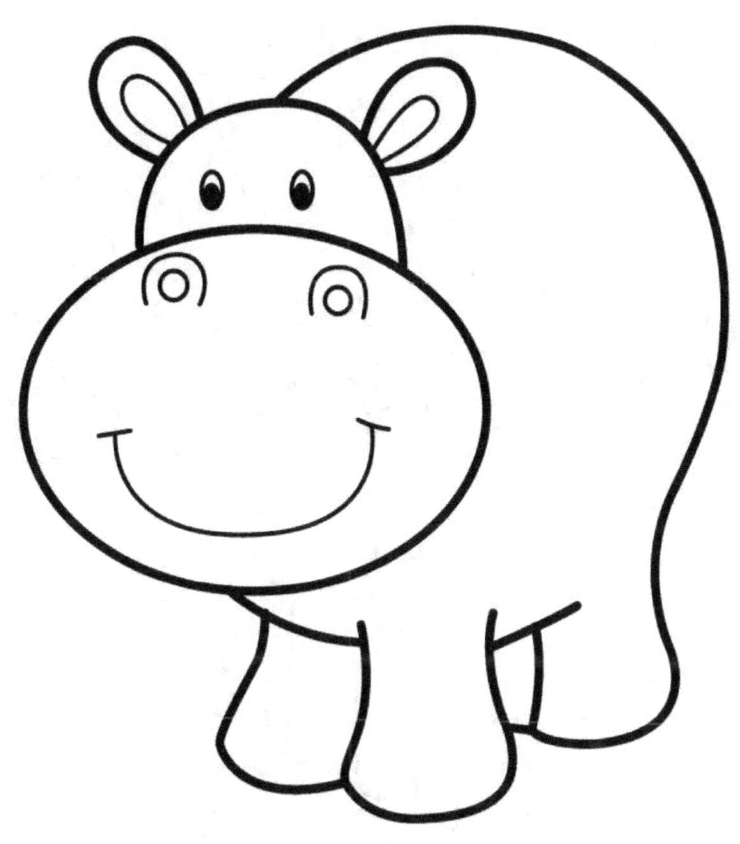

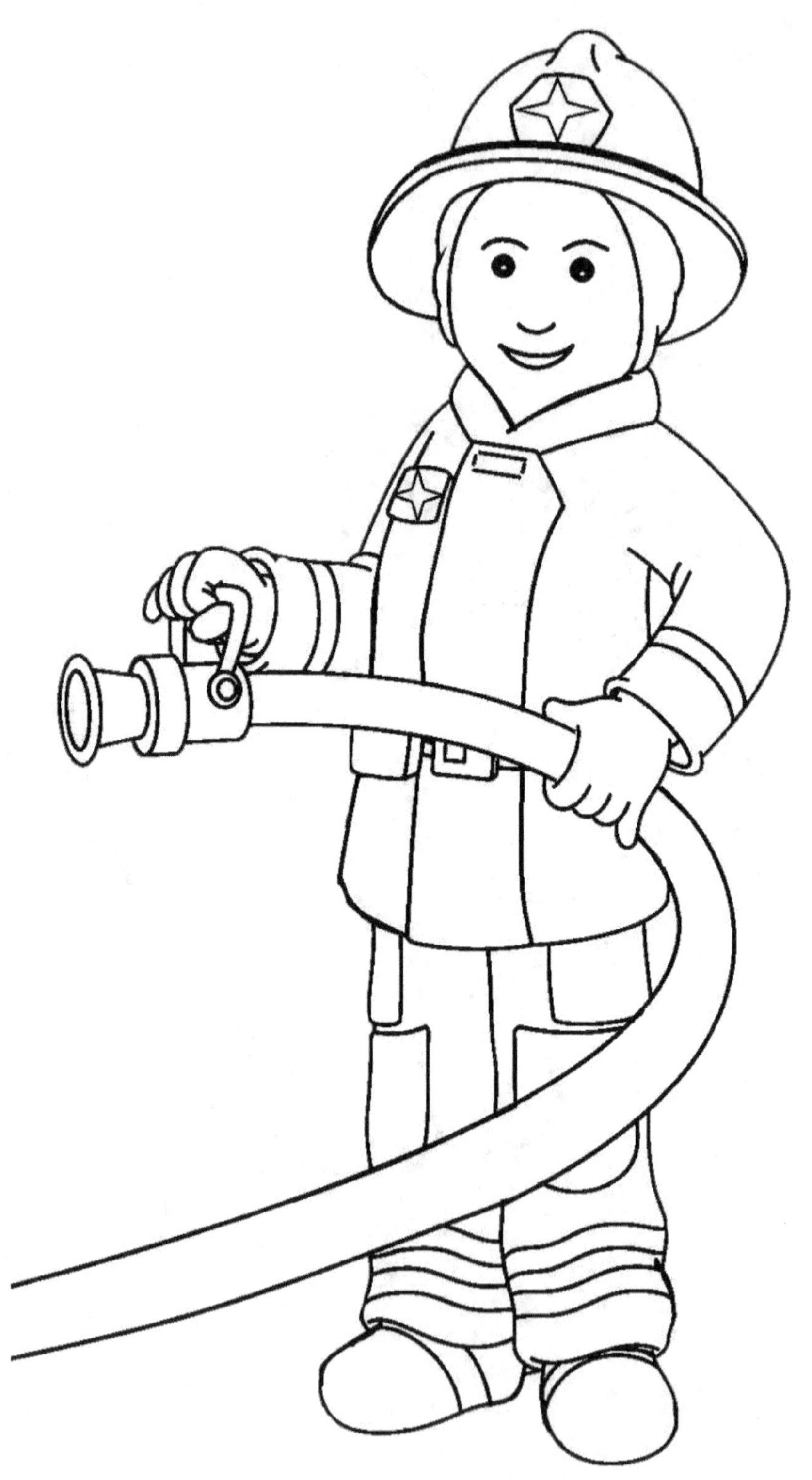

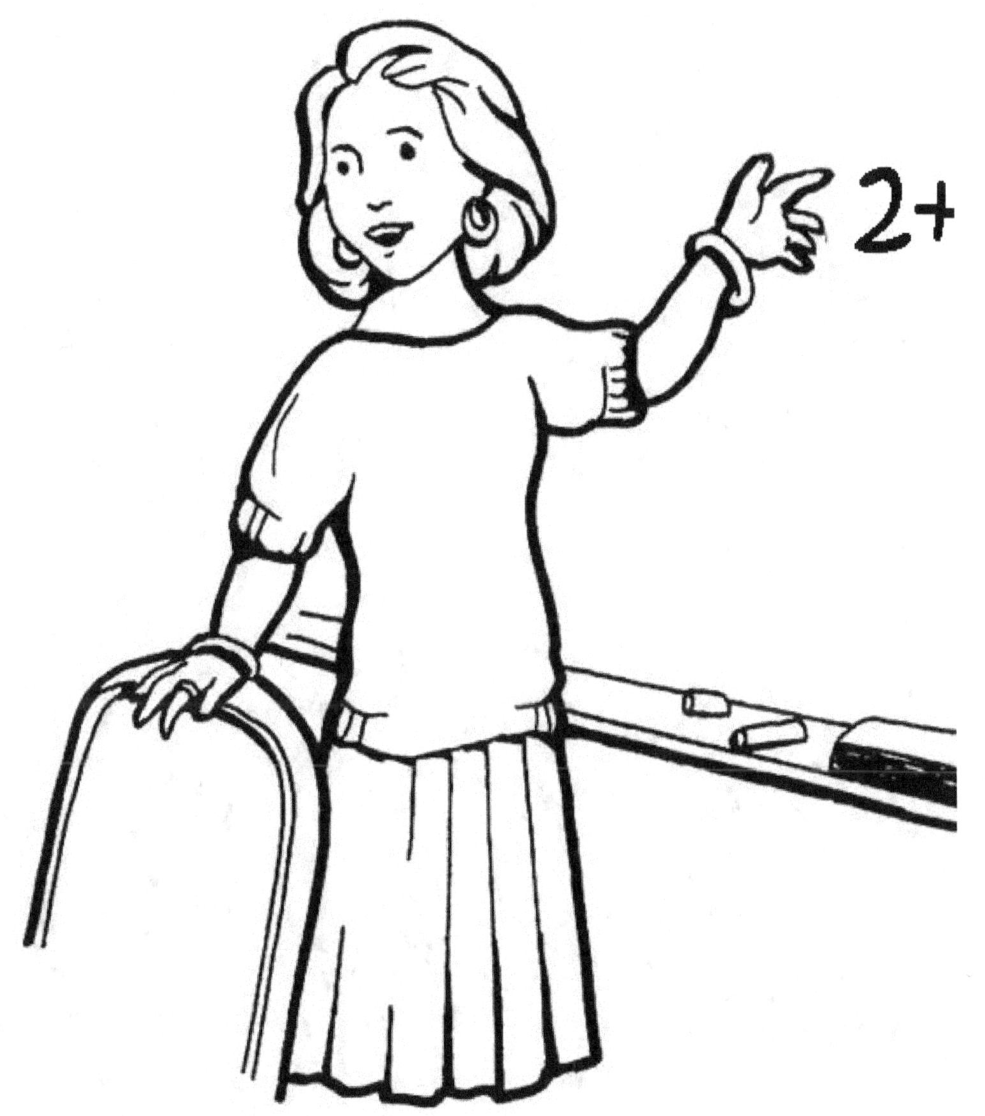

2+

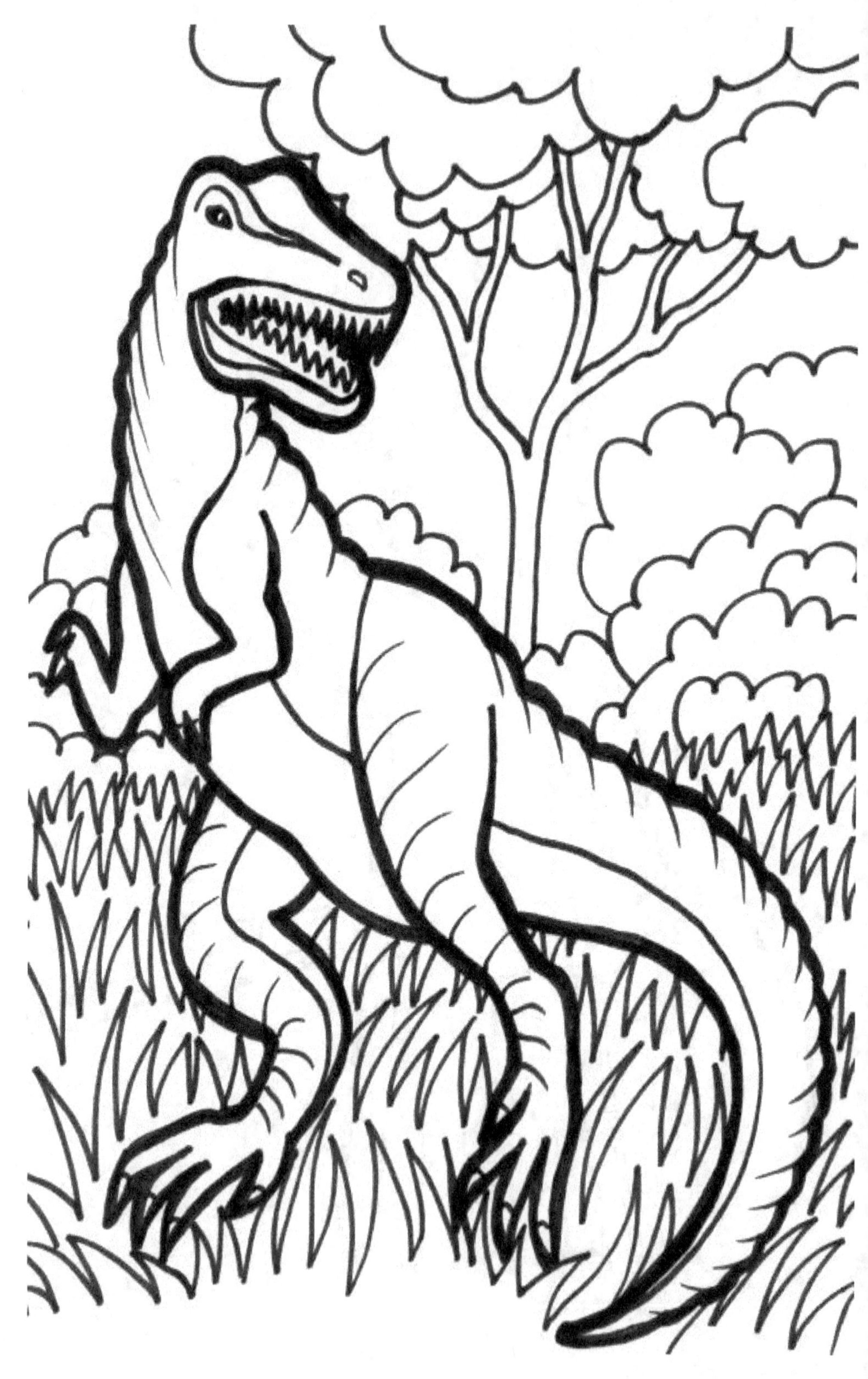

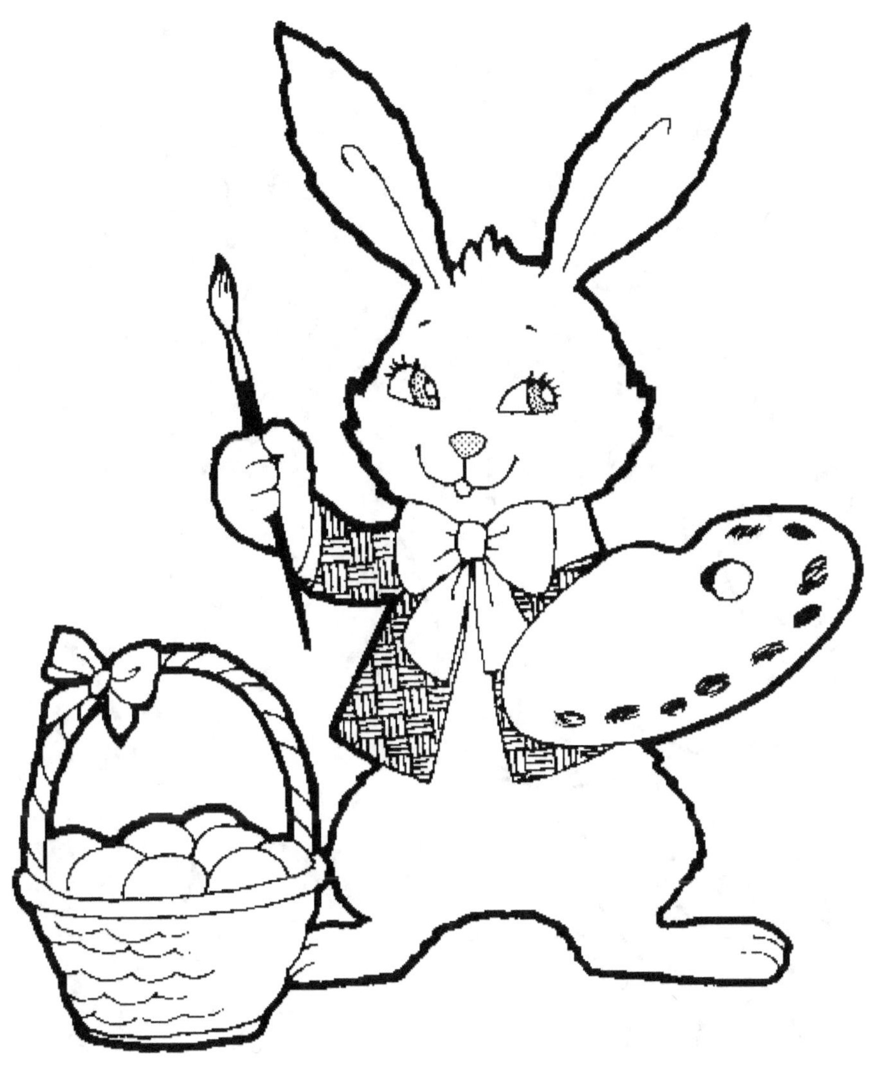

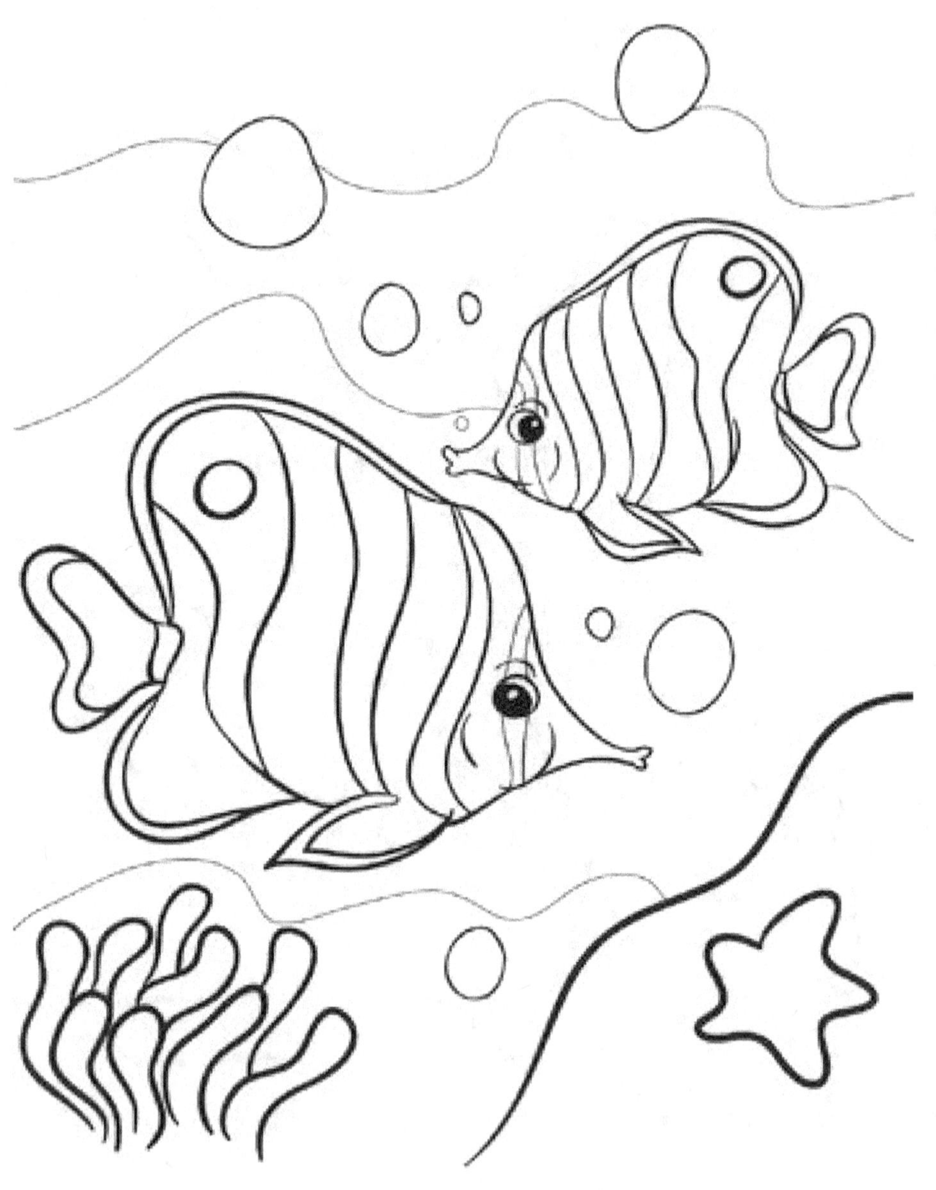

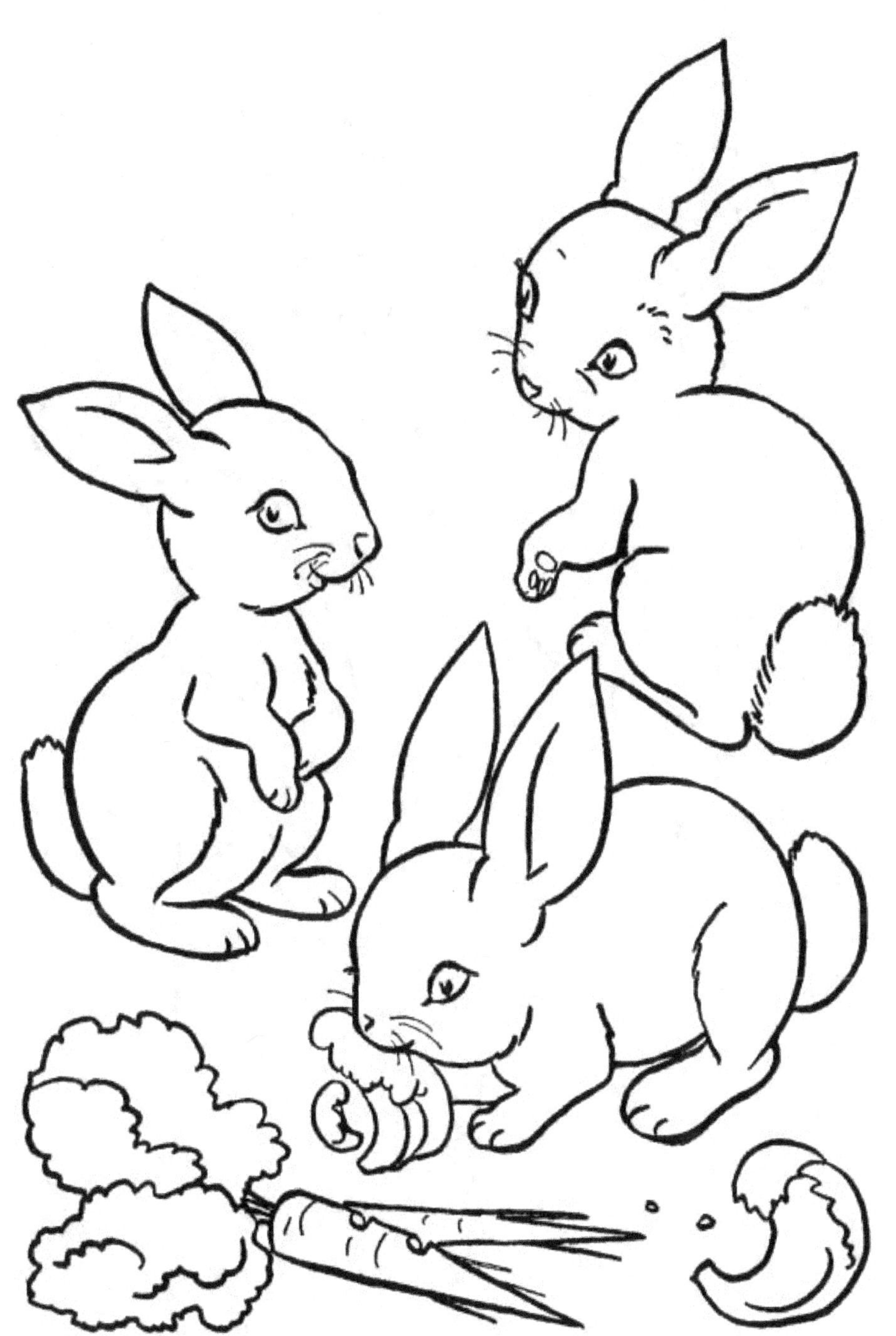

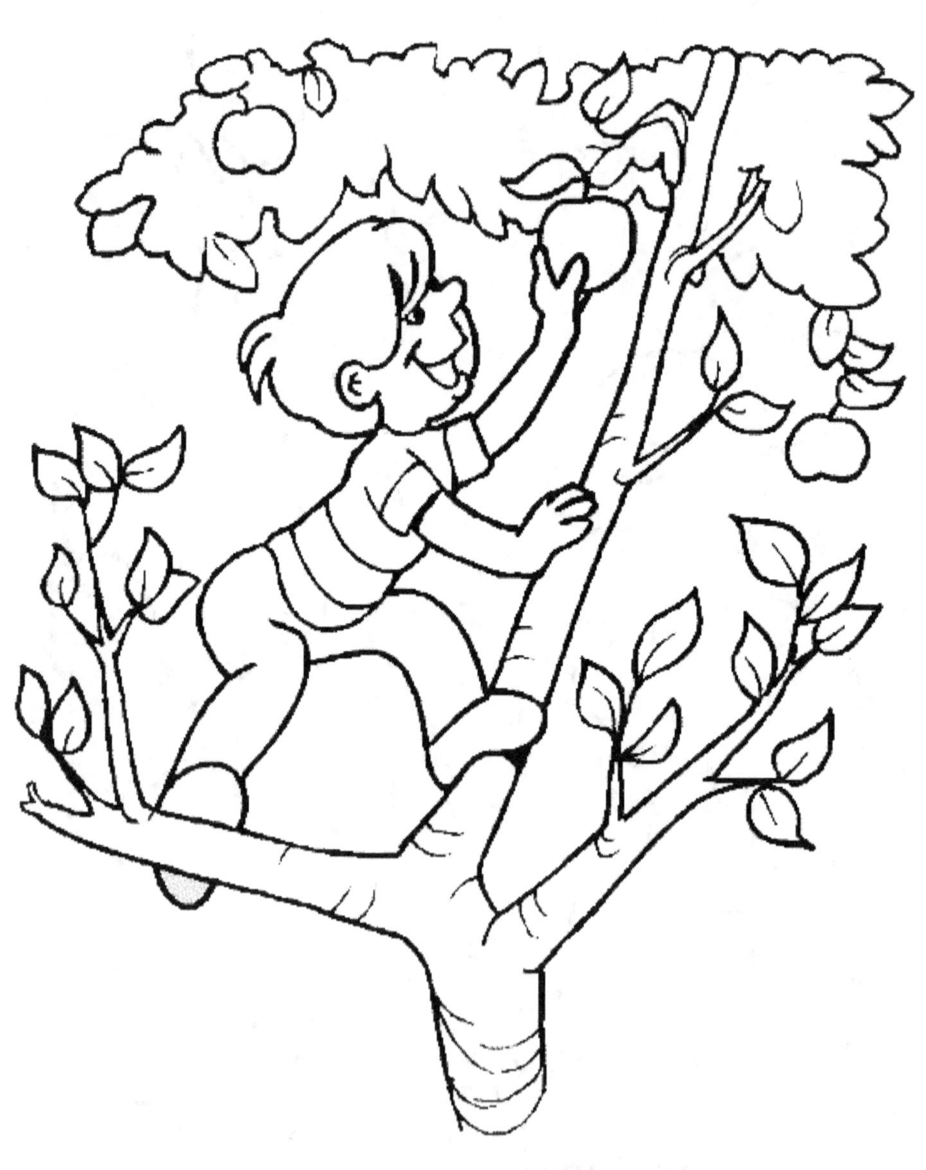

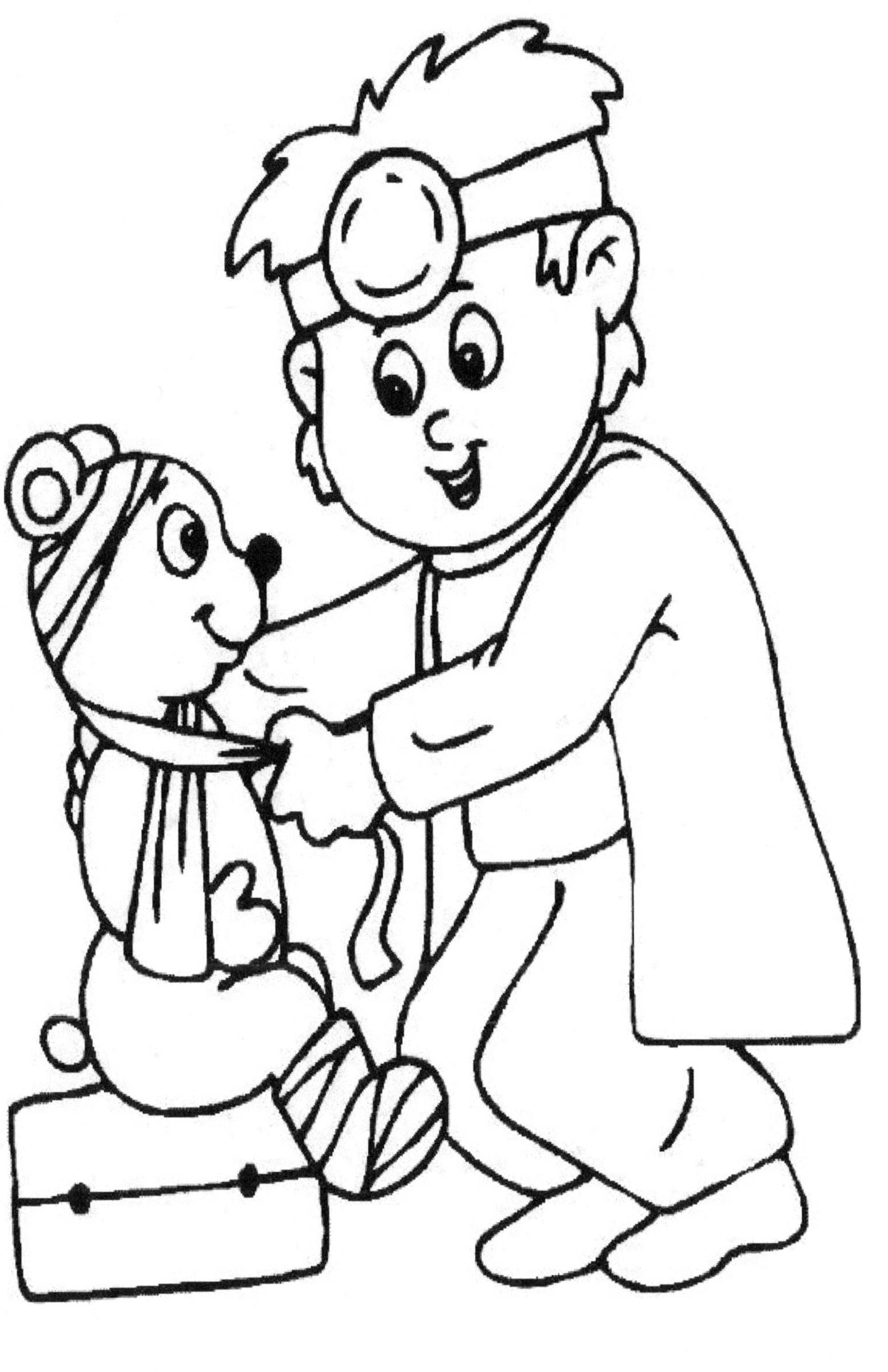

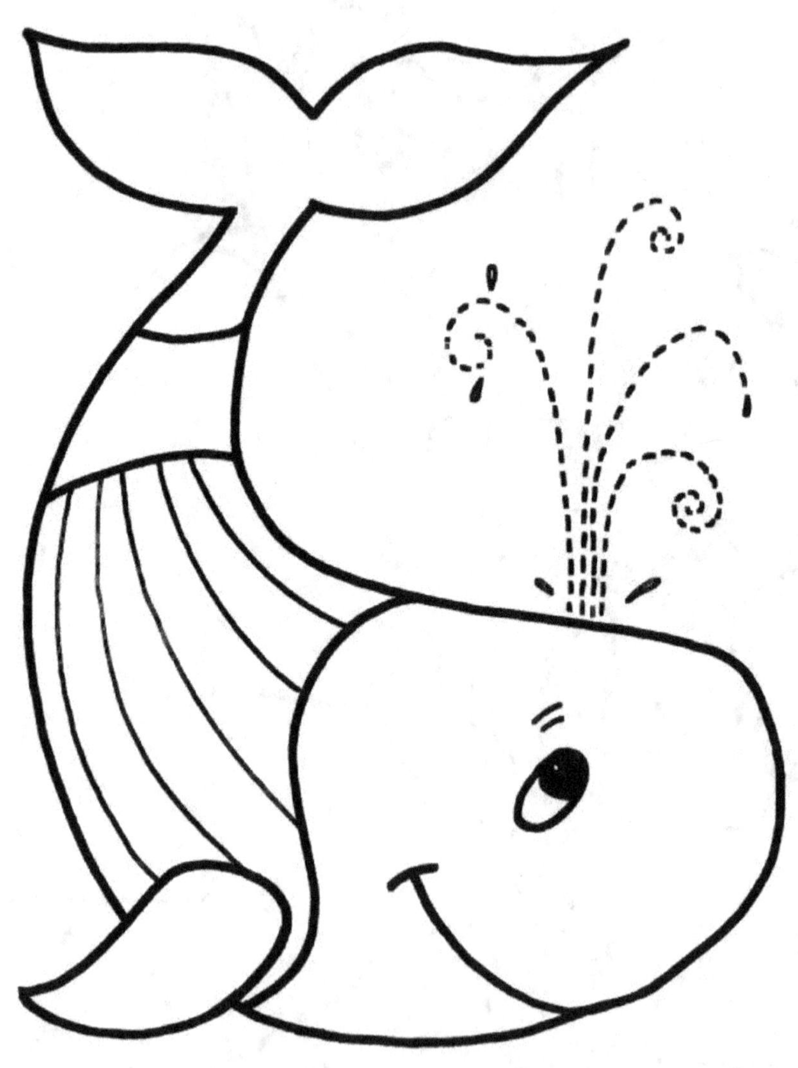

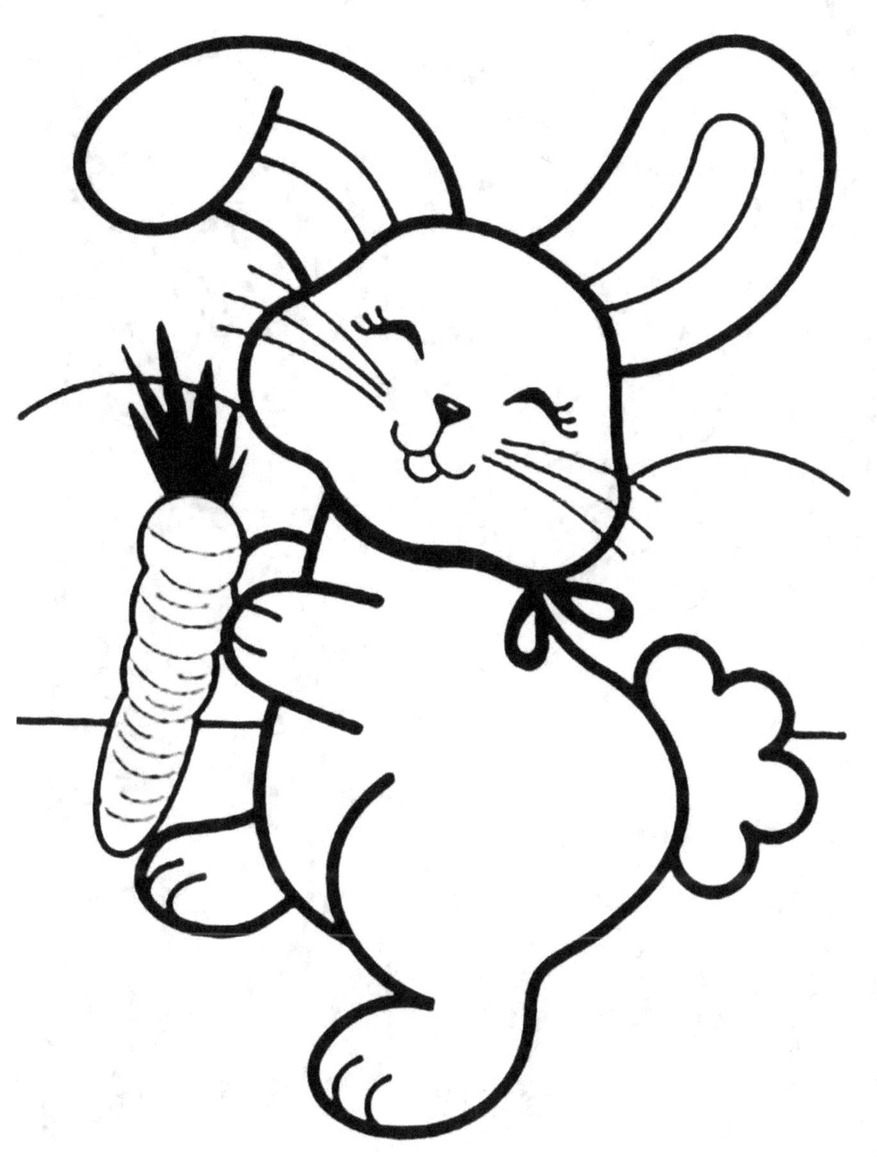

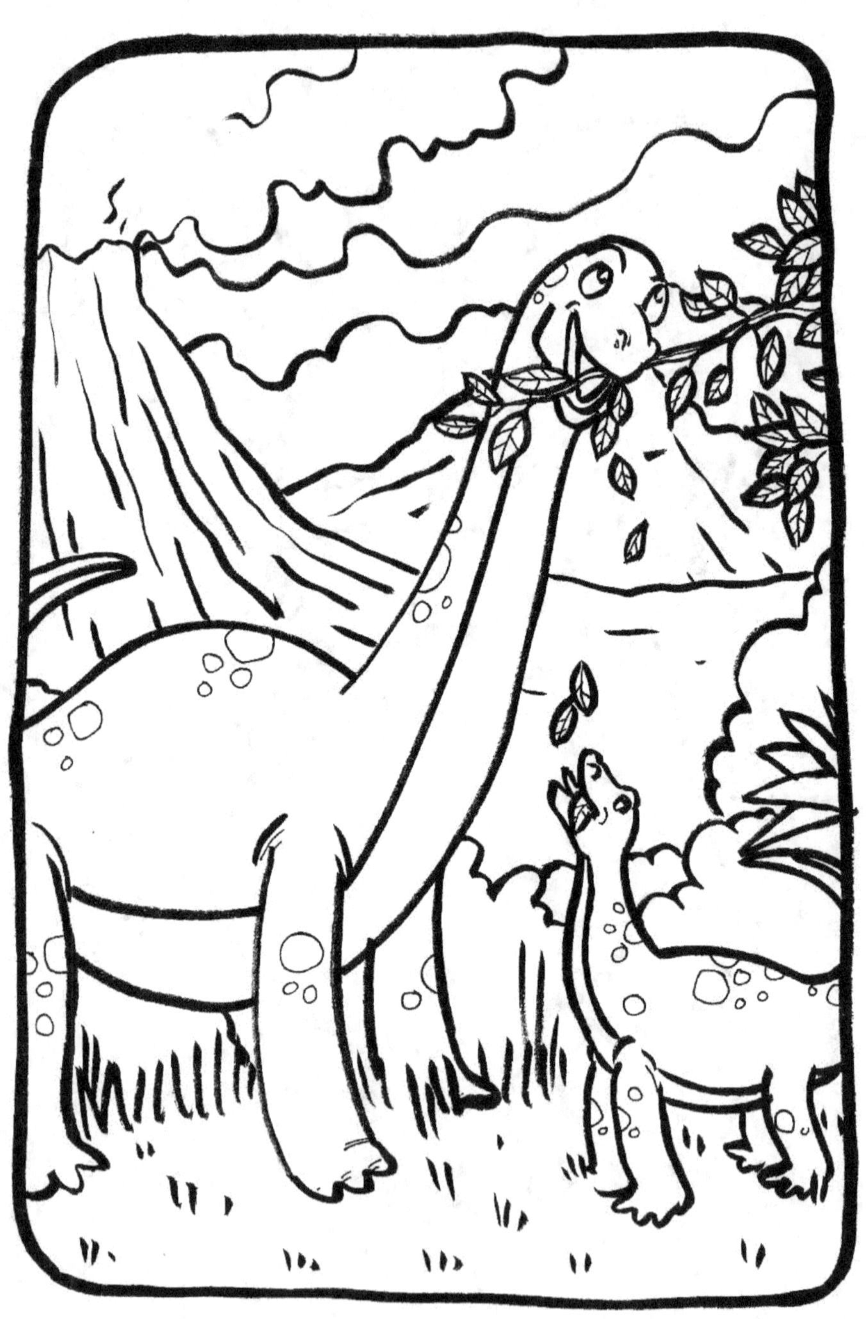

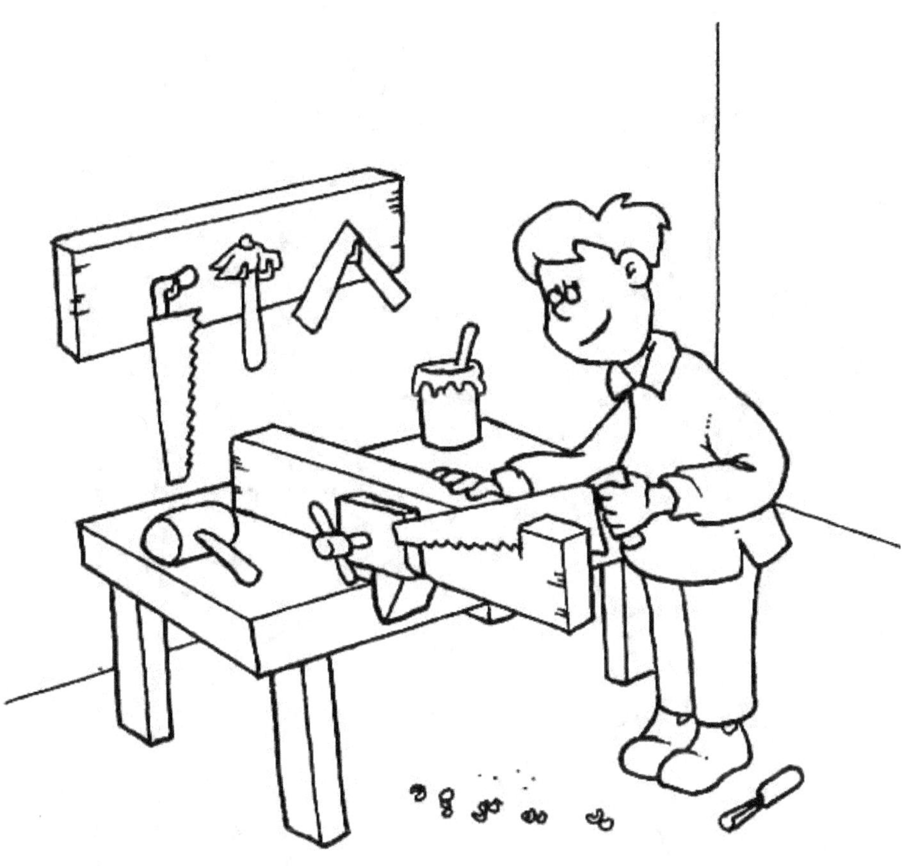

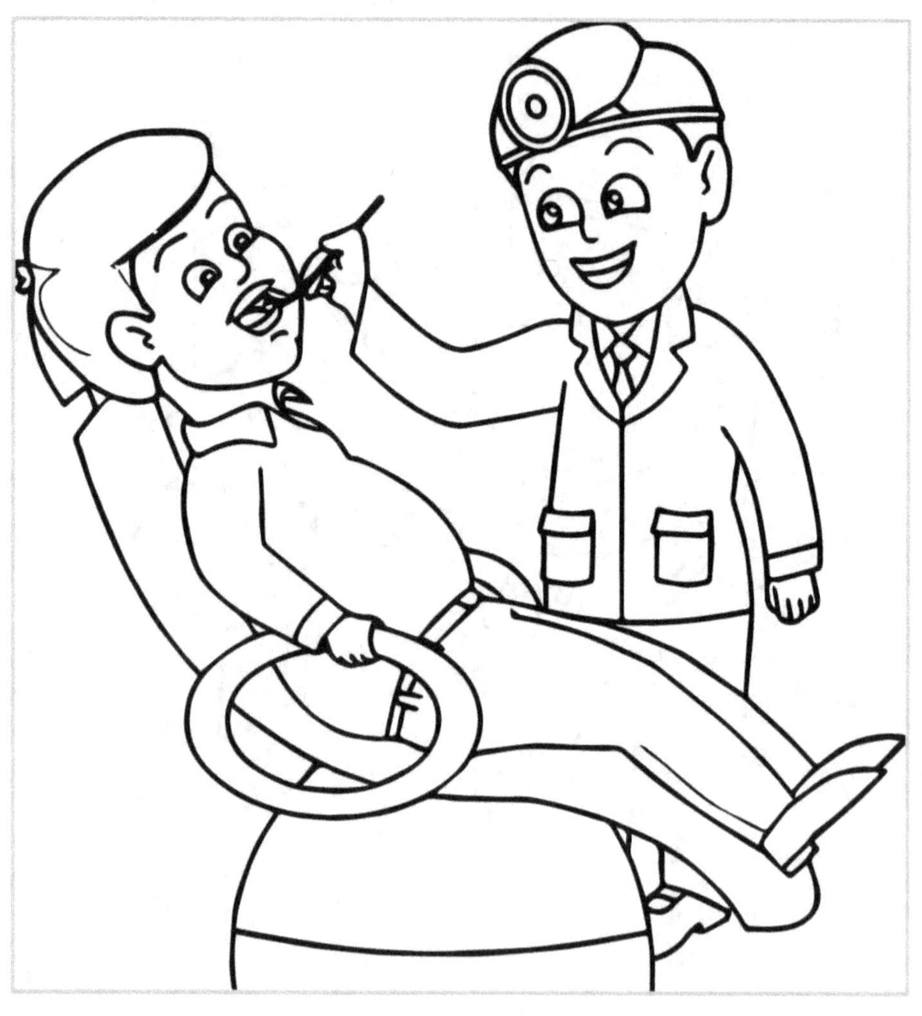

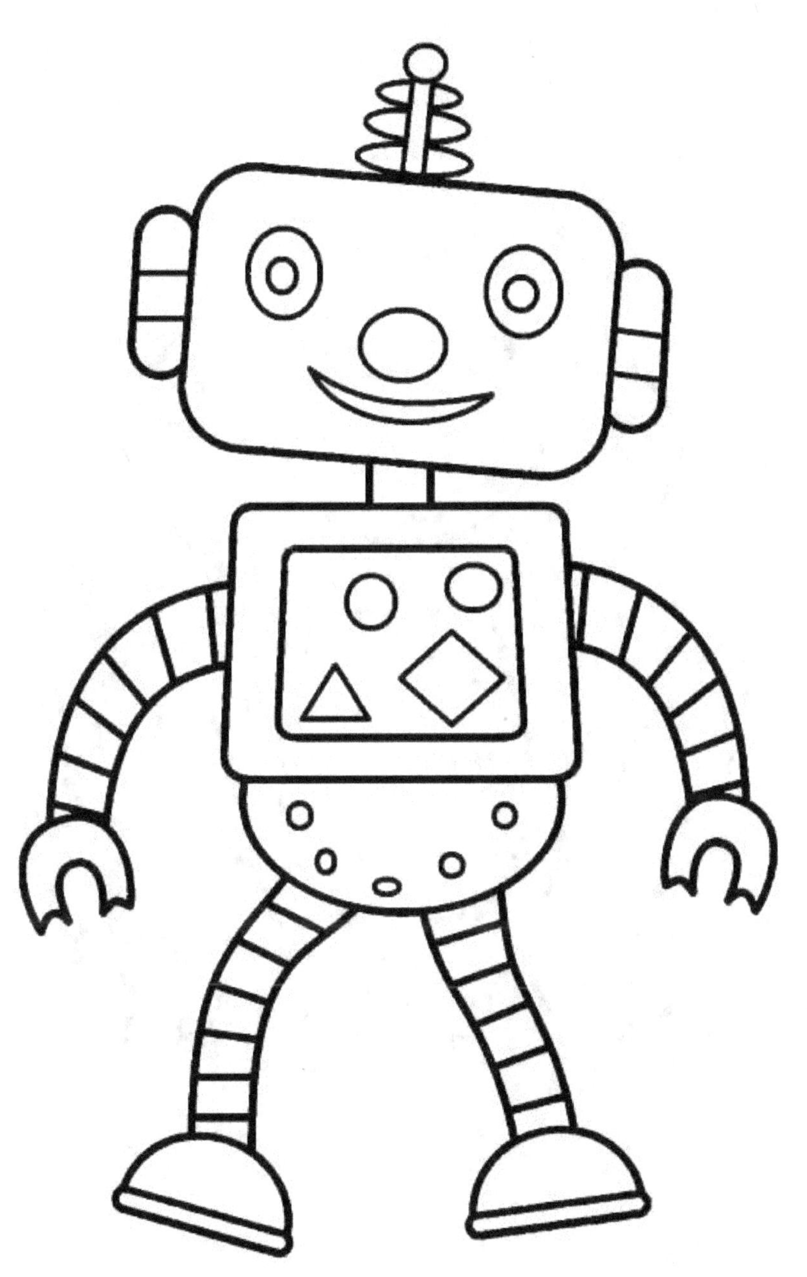

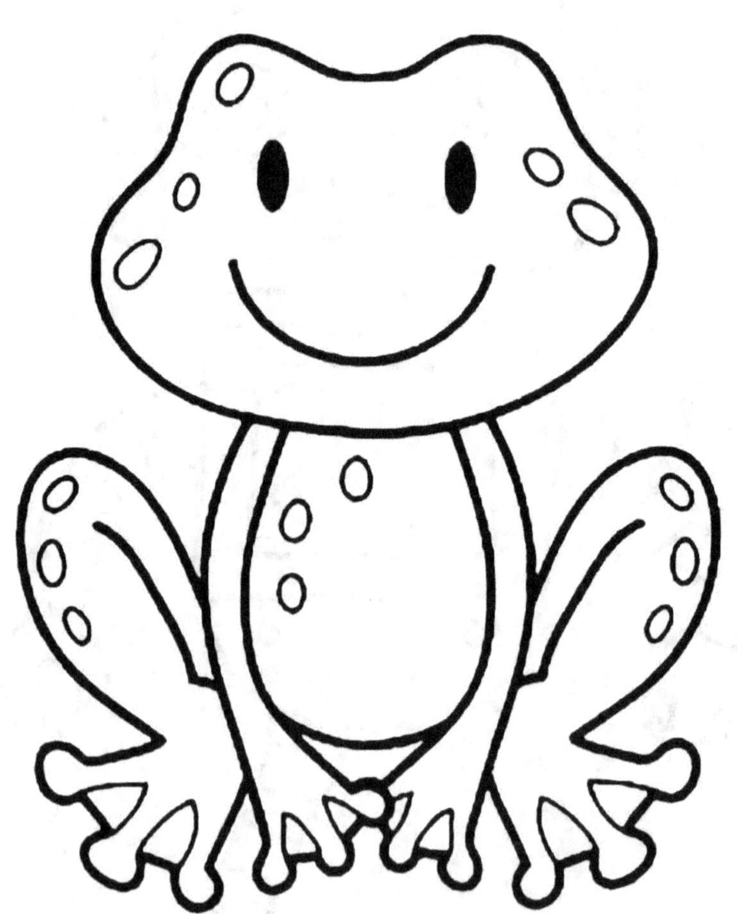

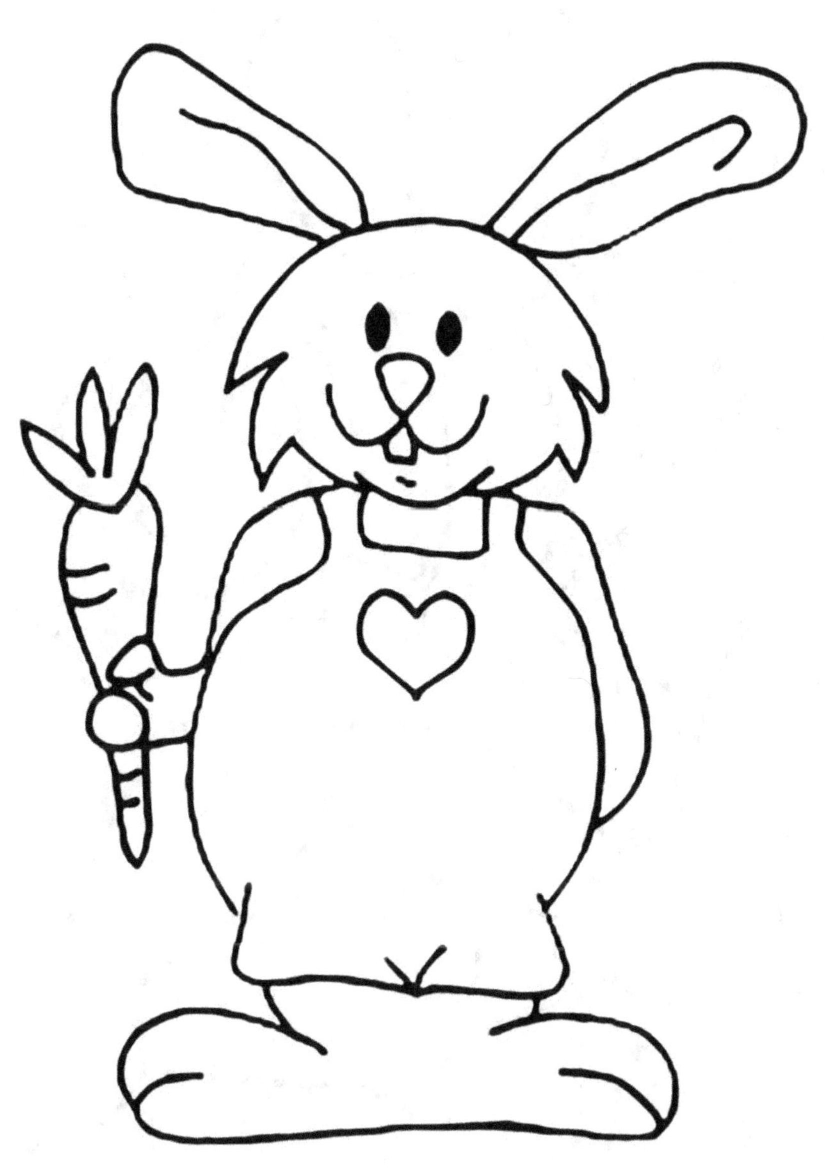

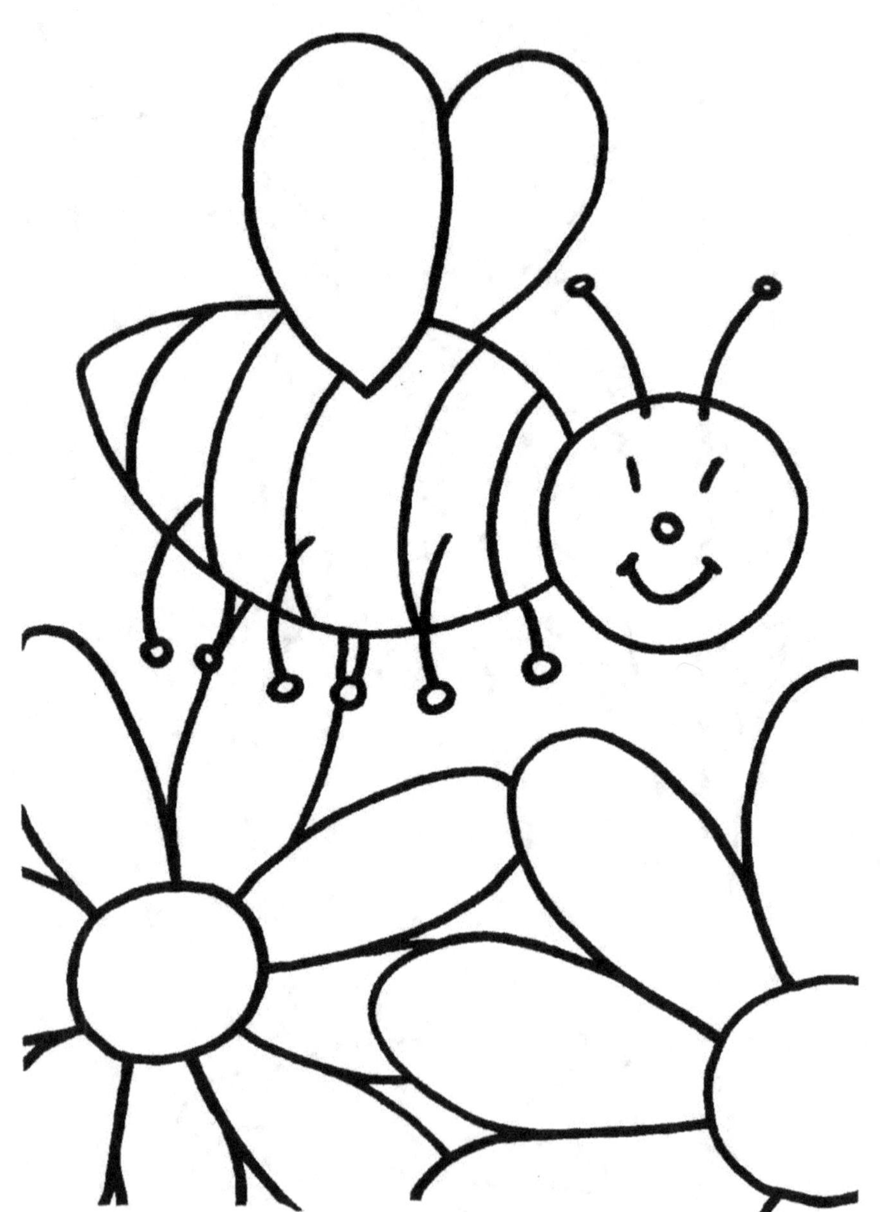

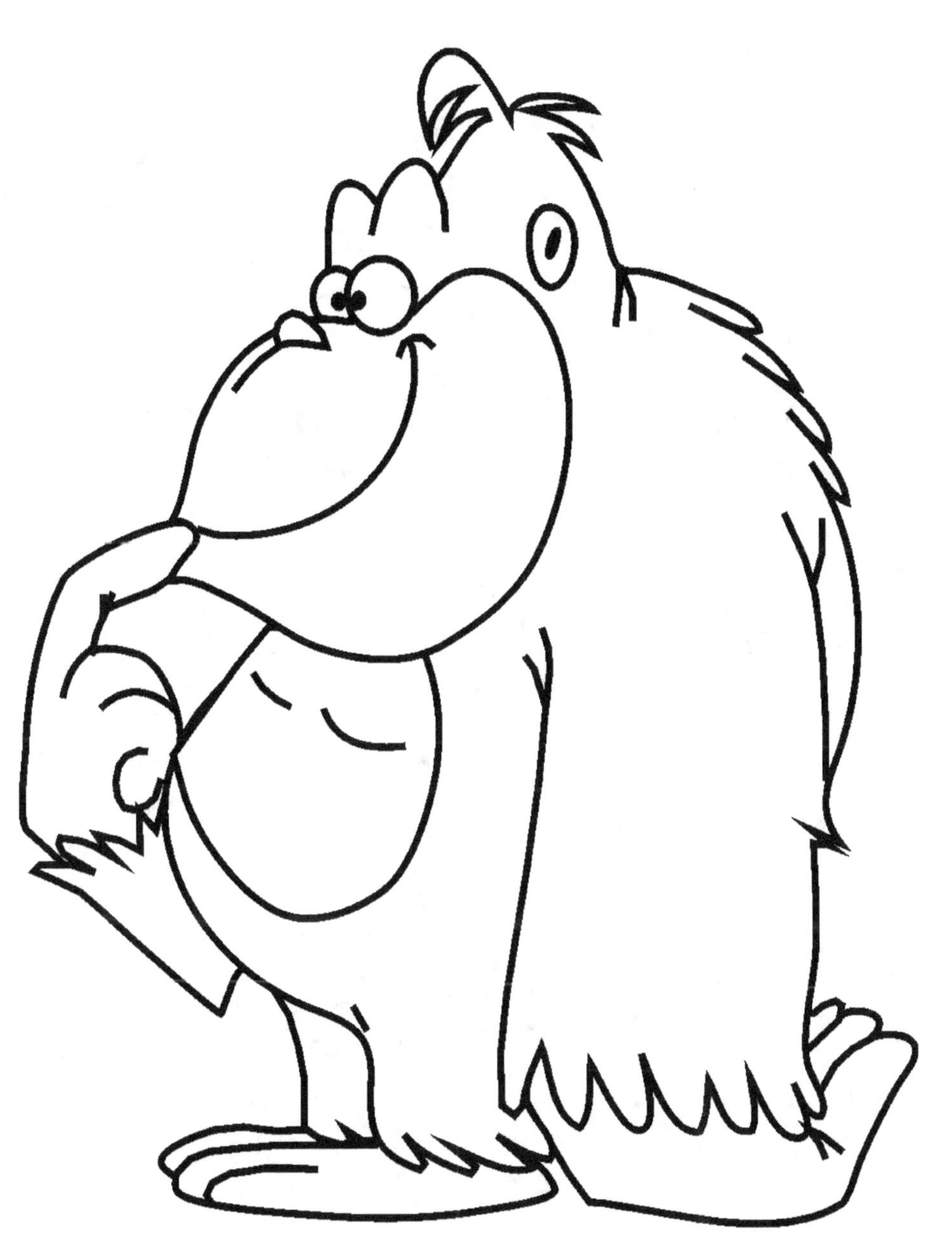

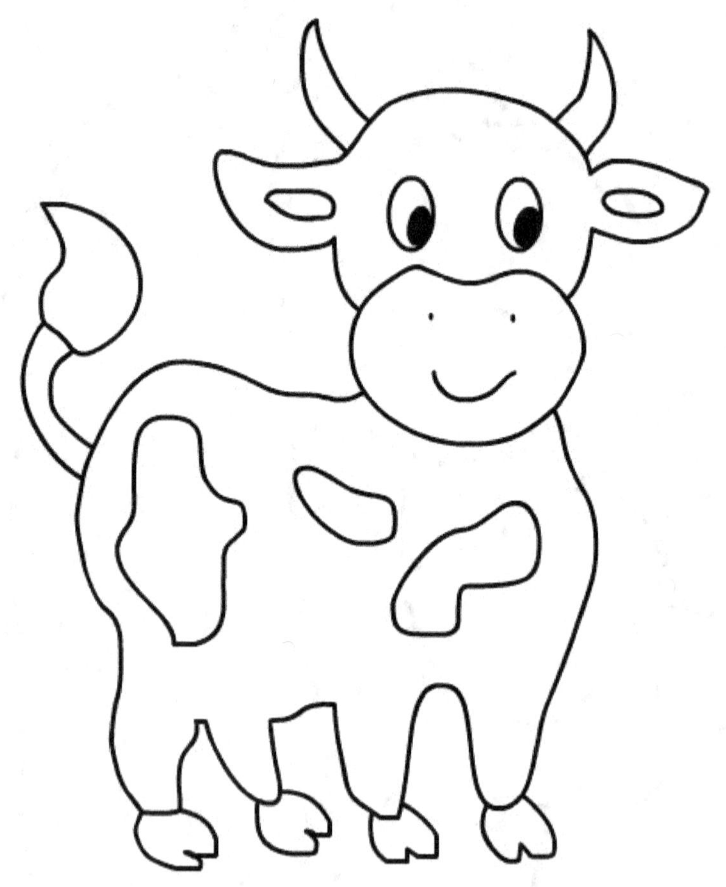

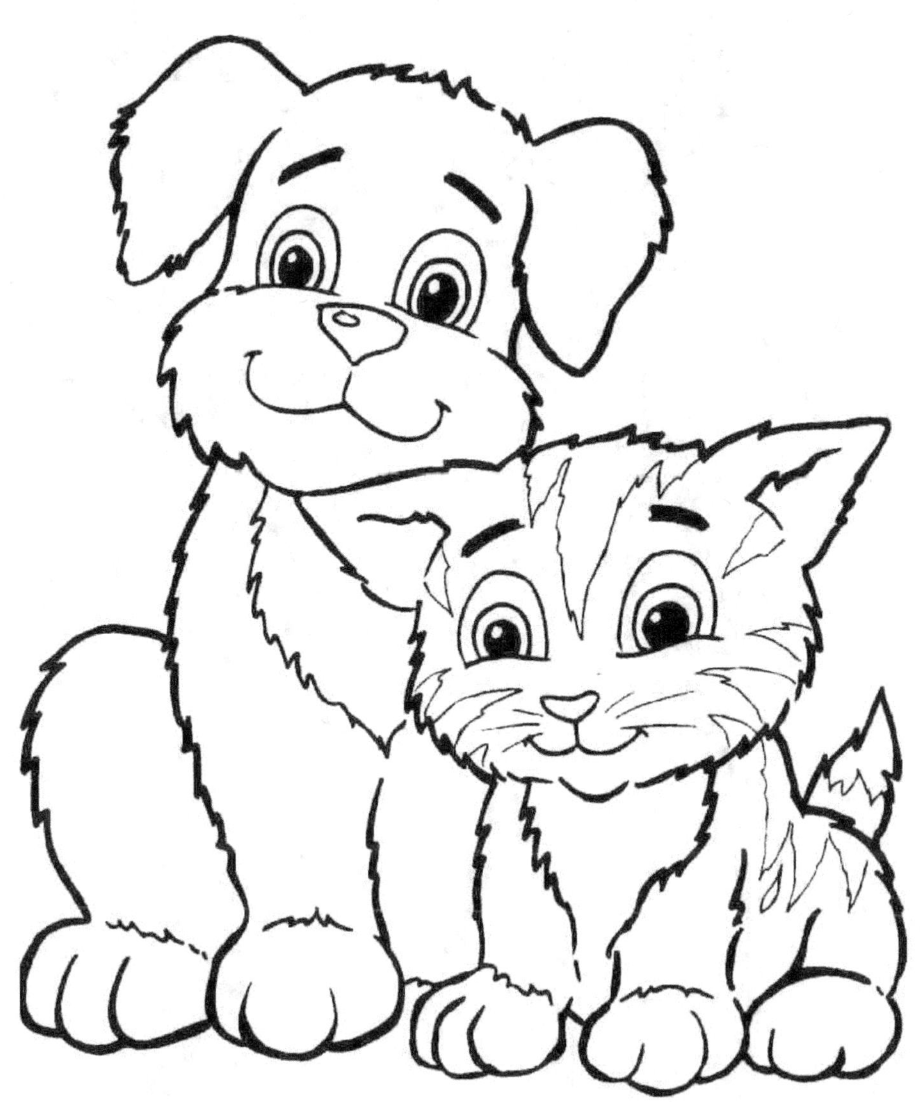

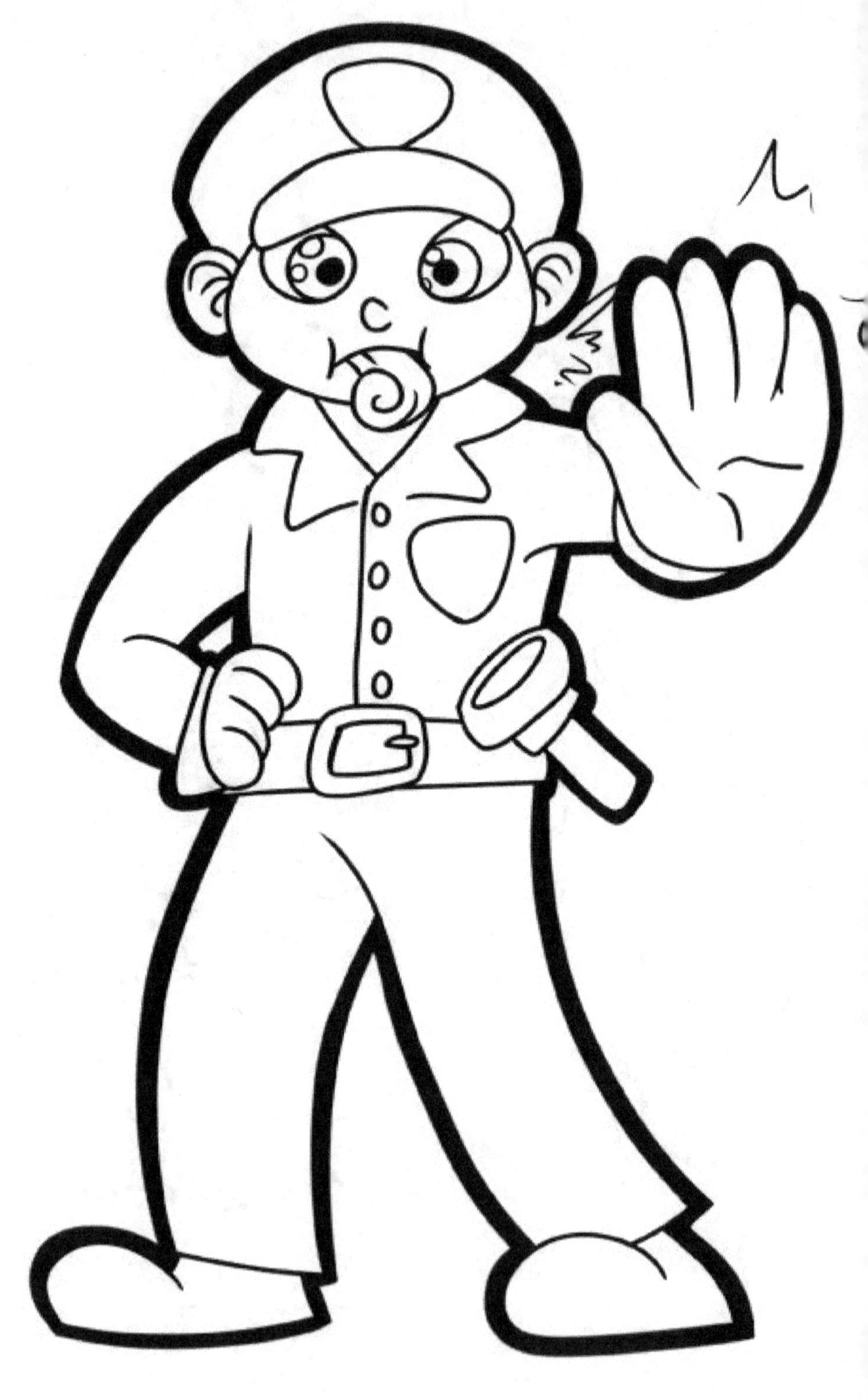

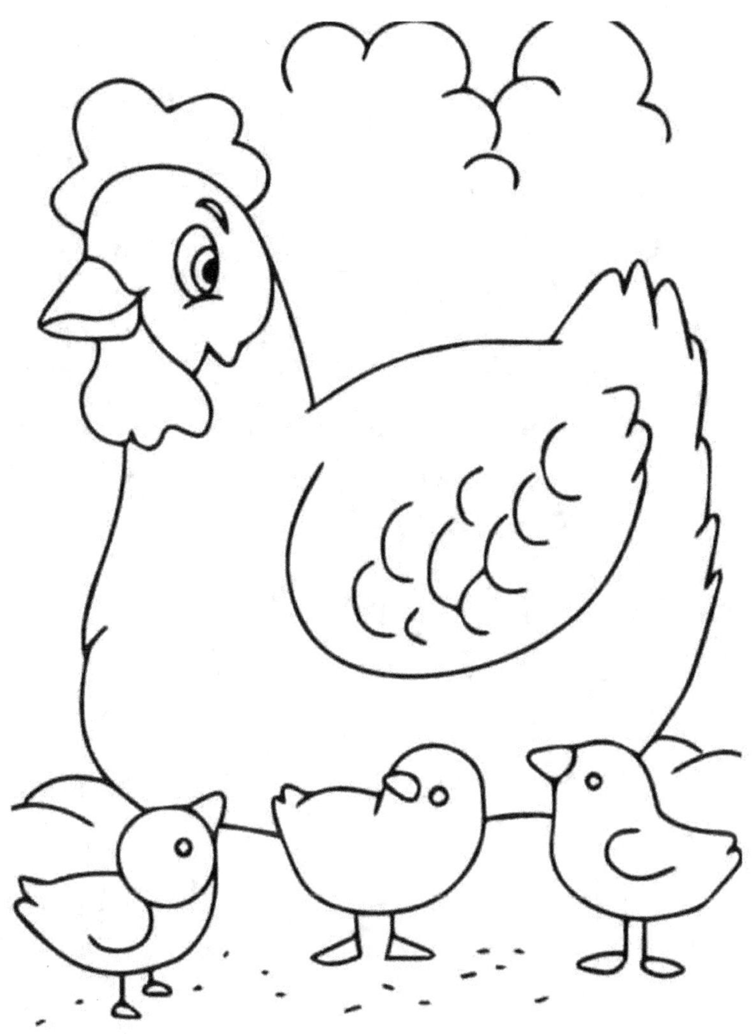

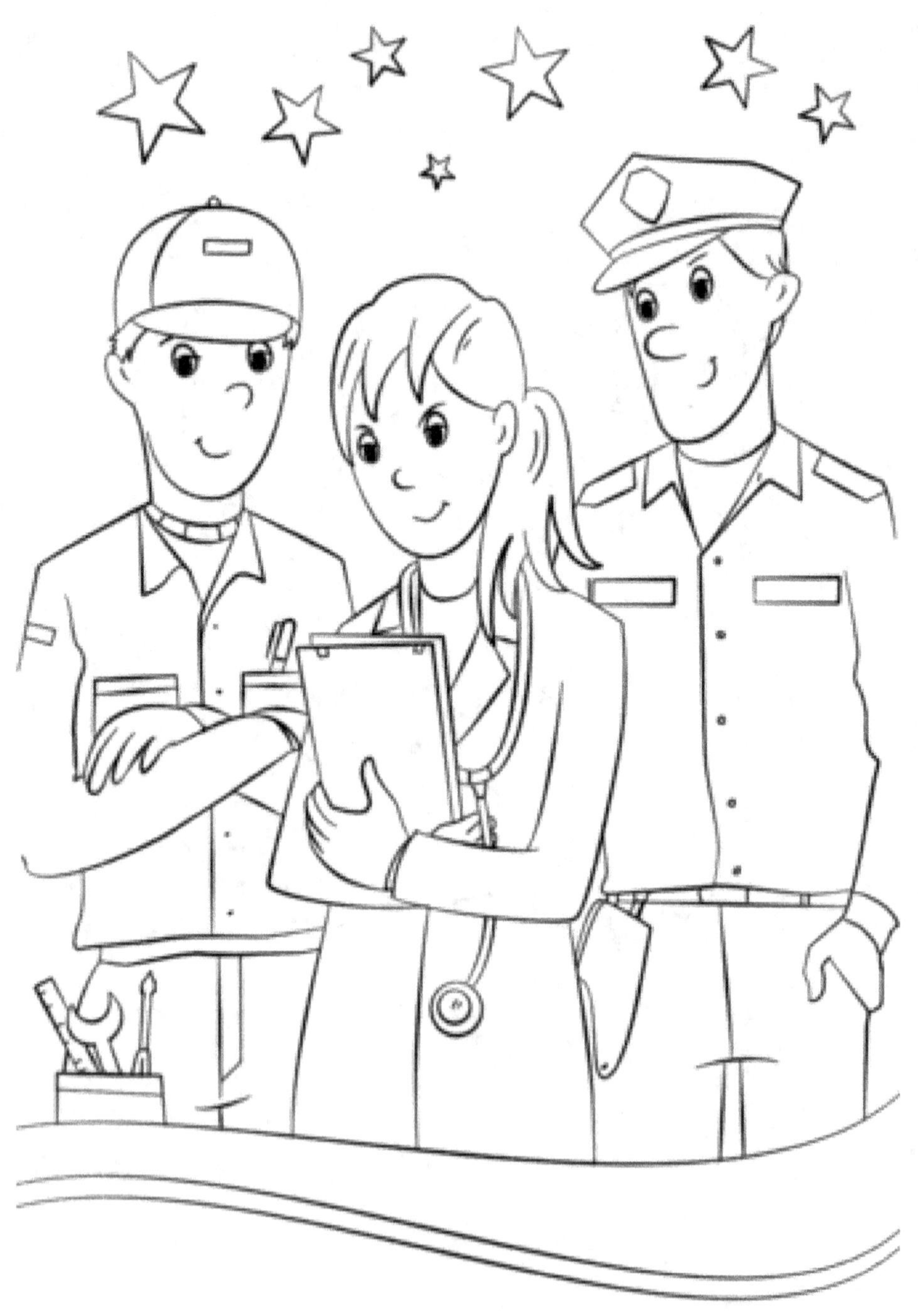

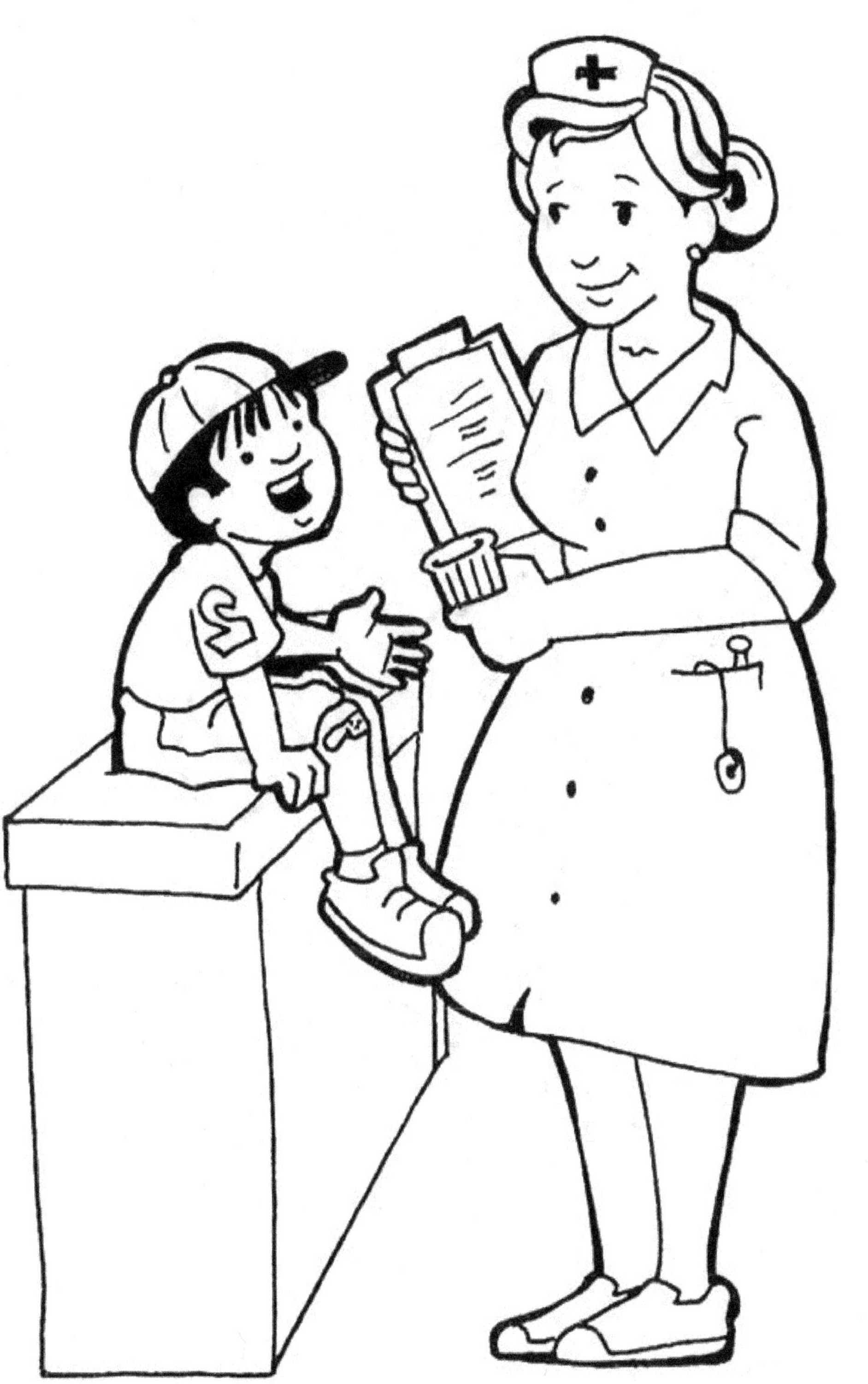

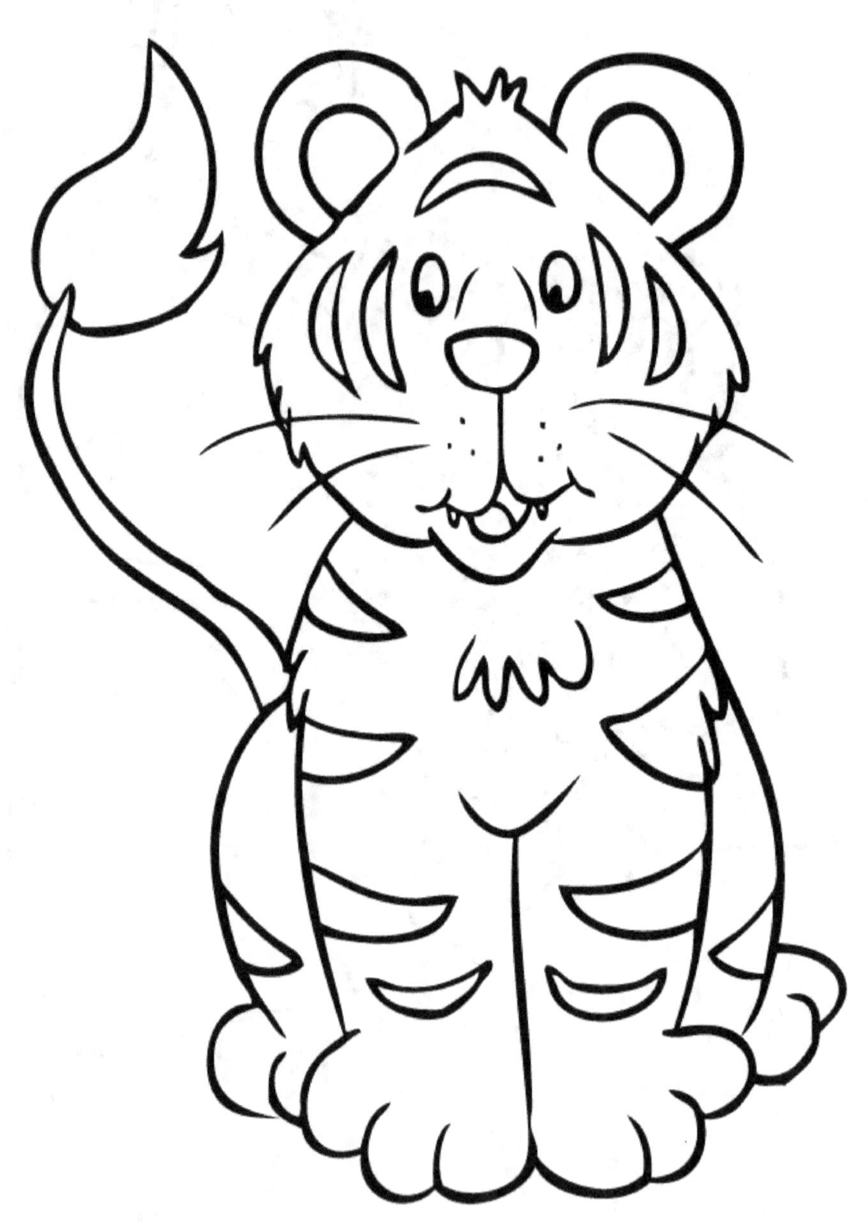

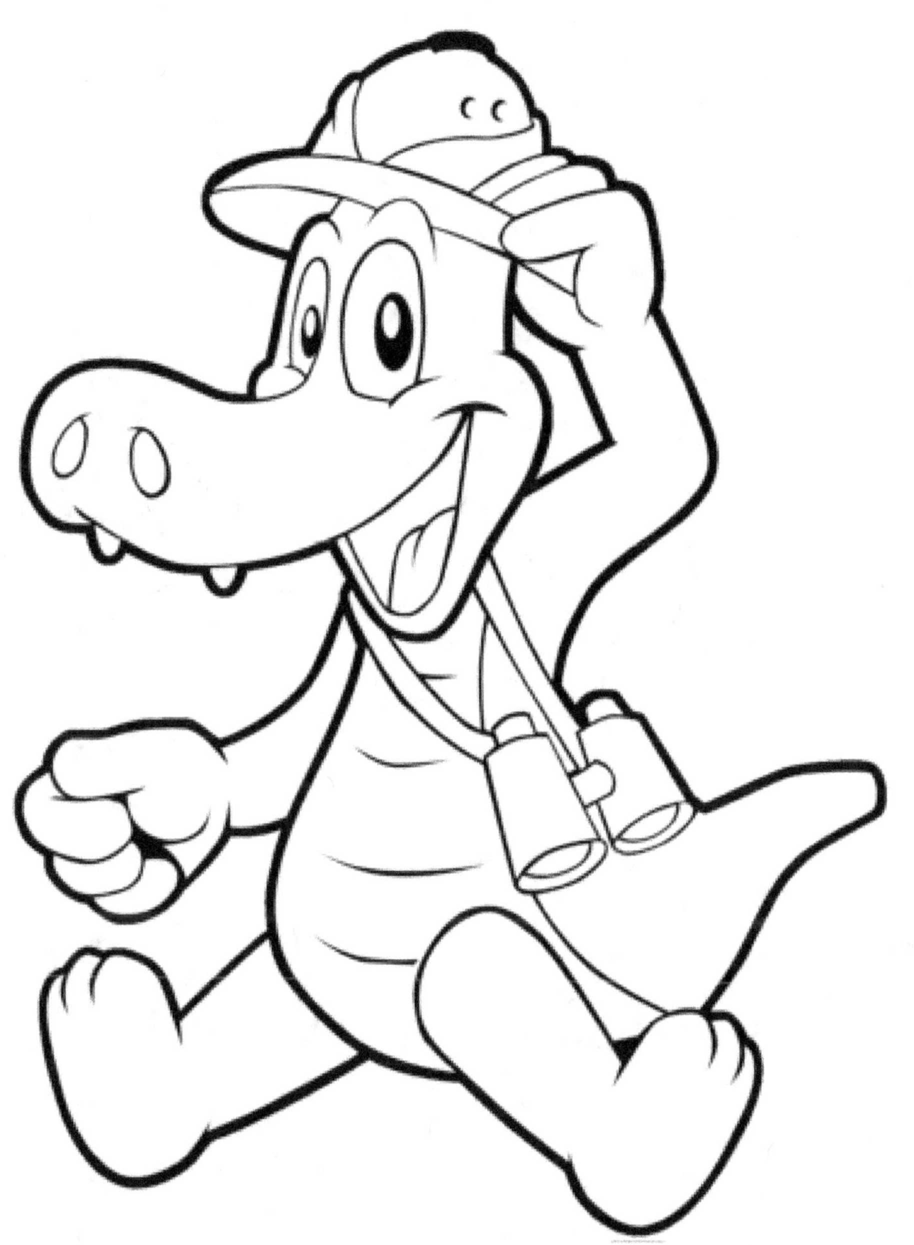

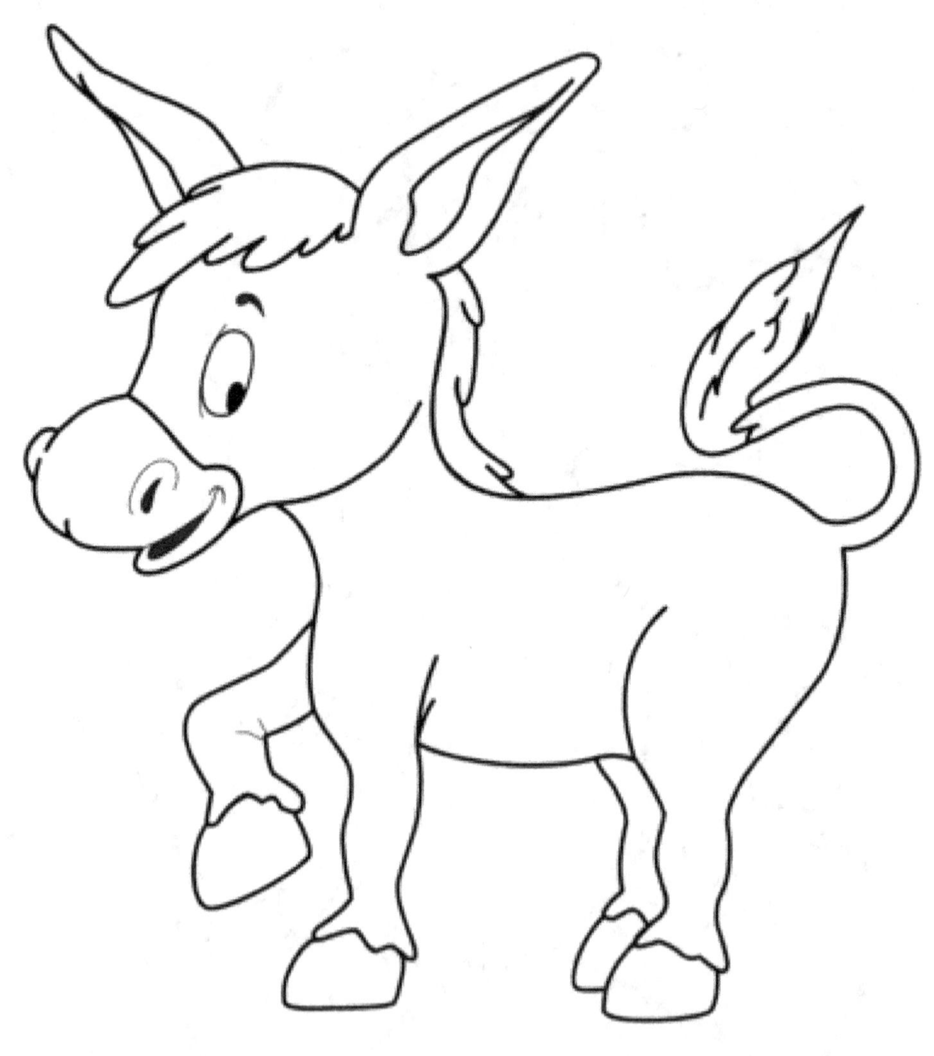

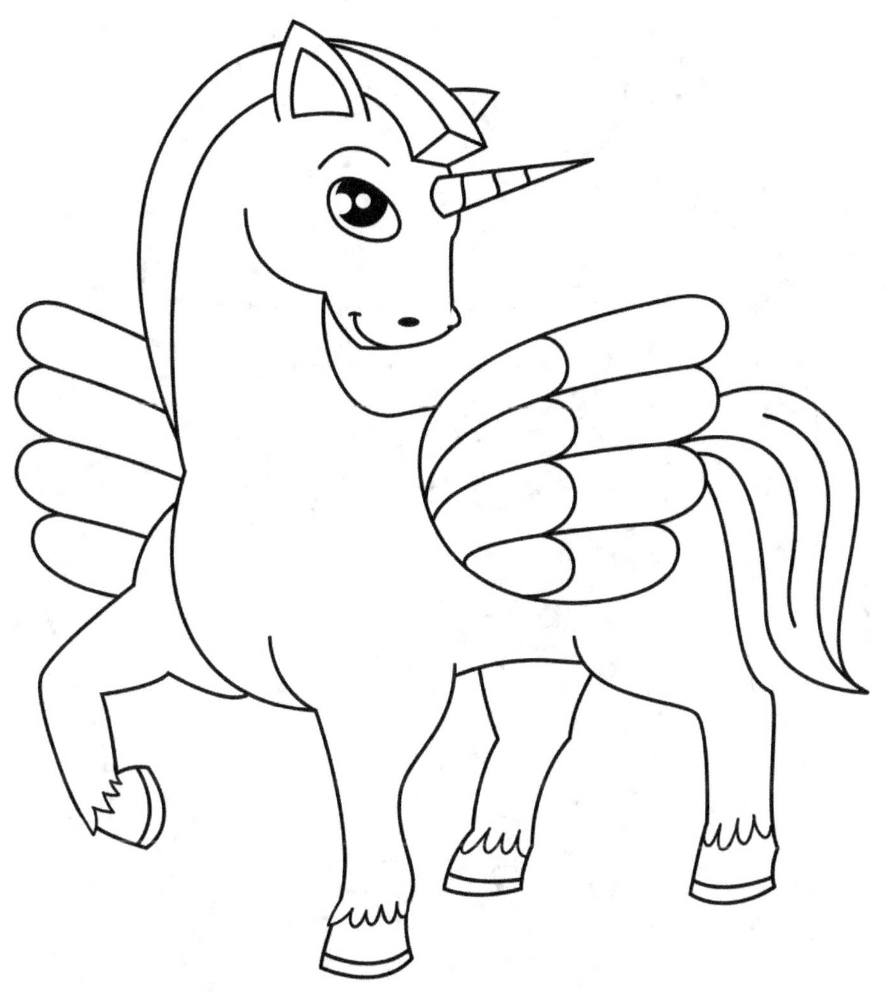

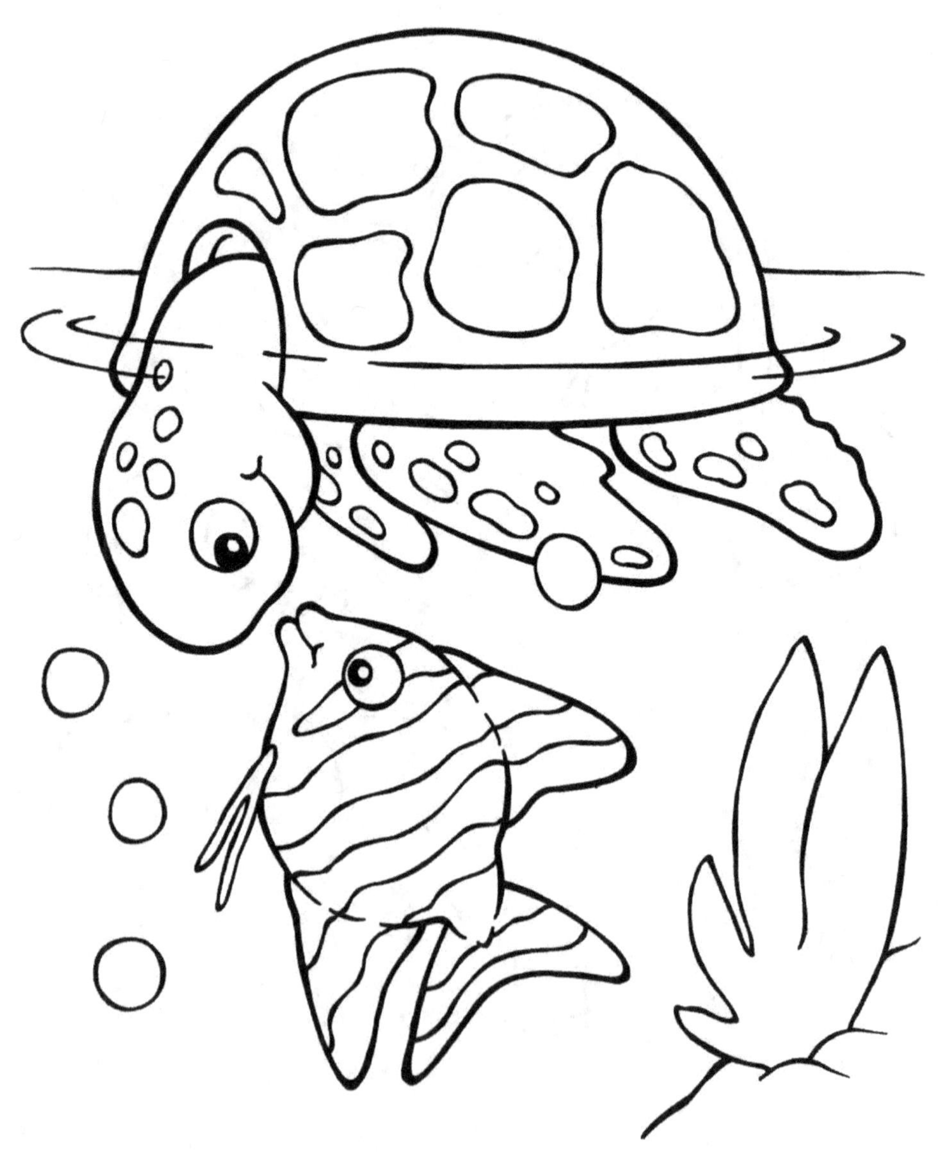

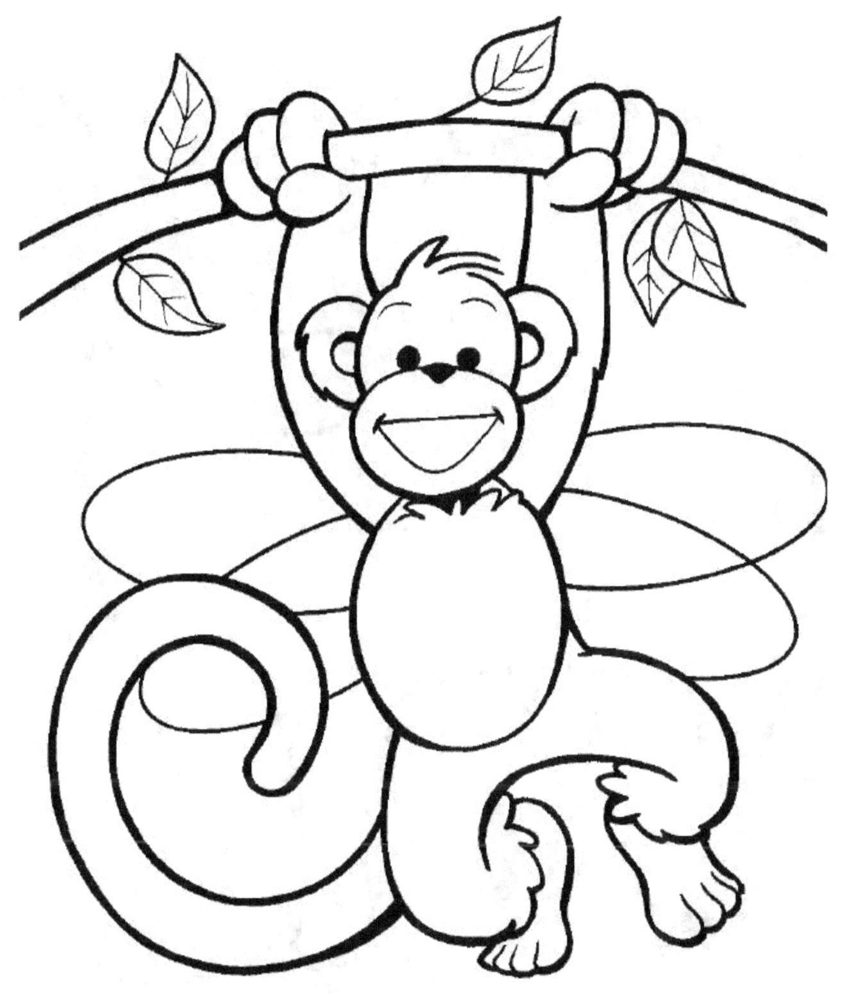

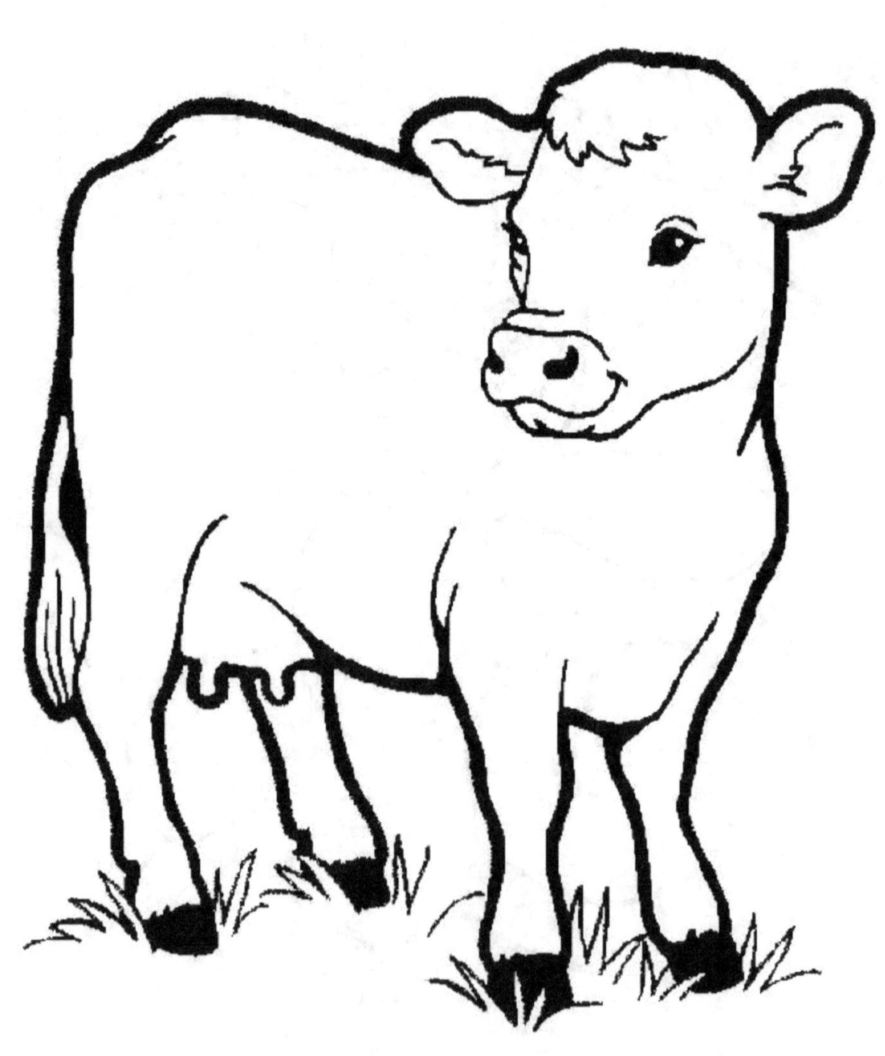

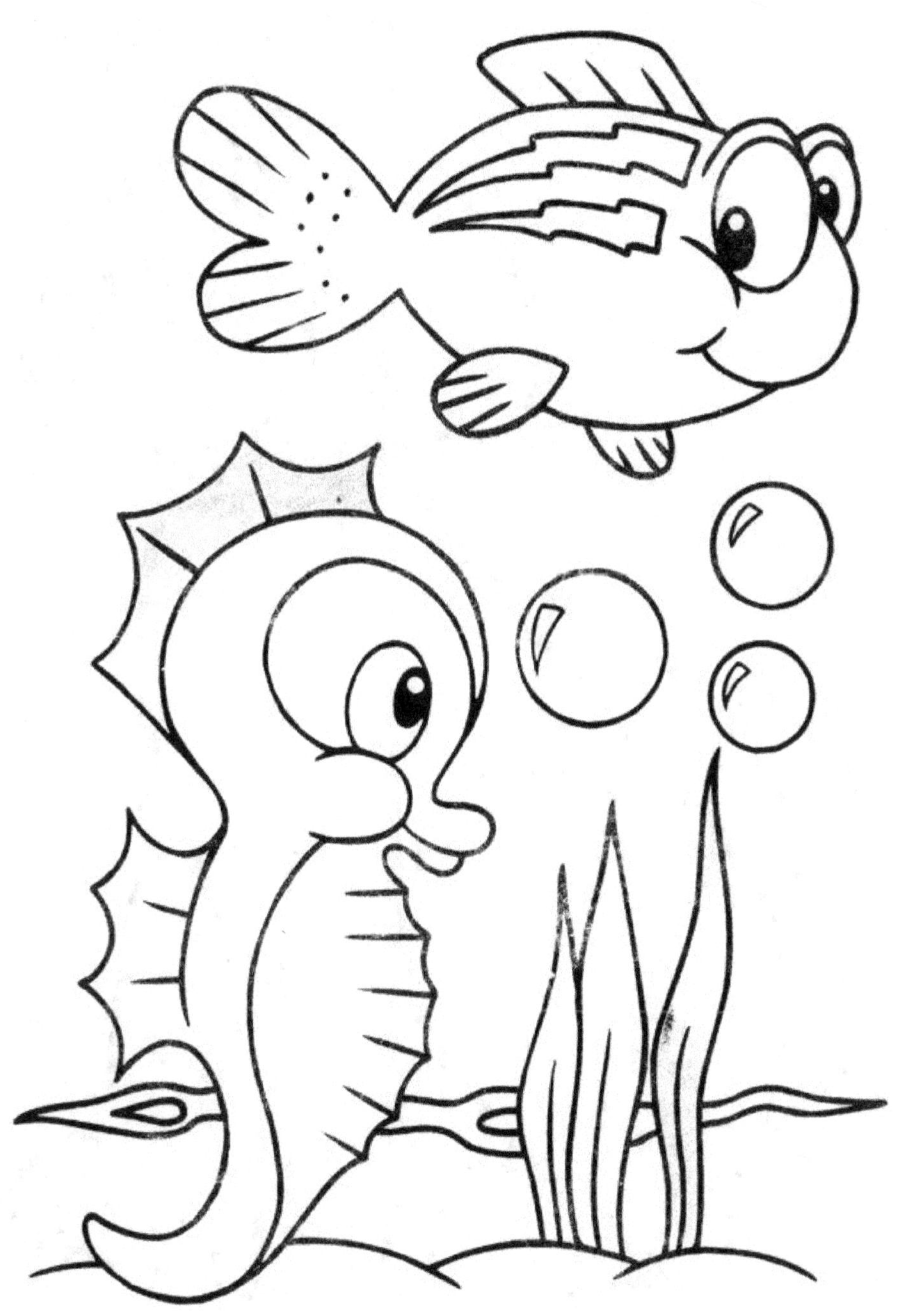

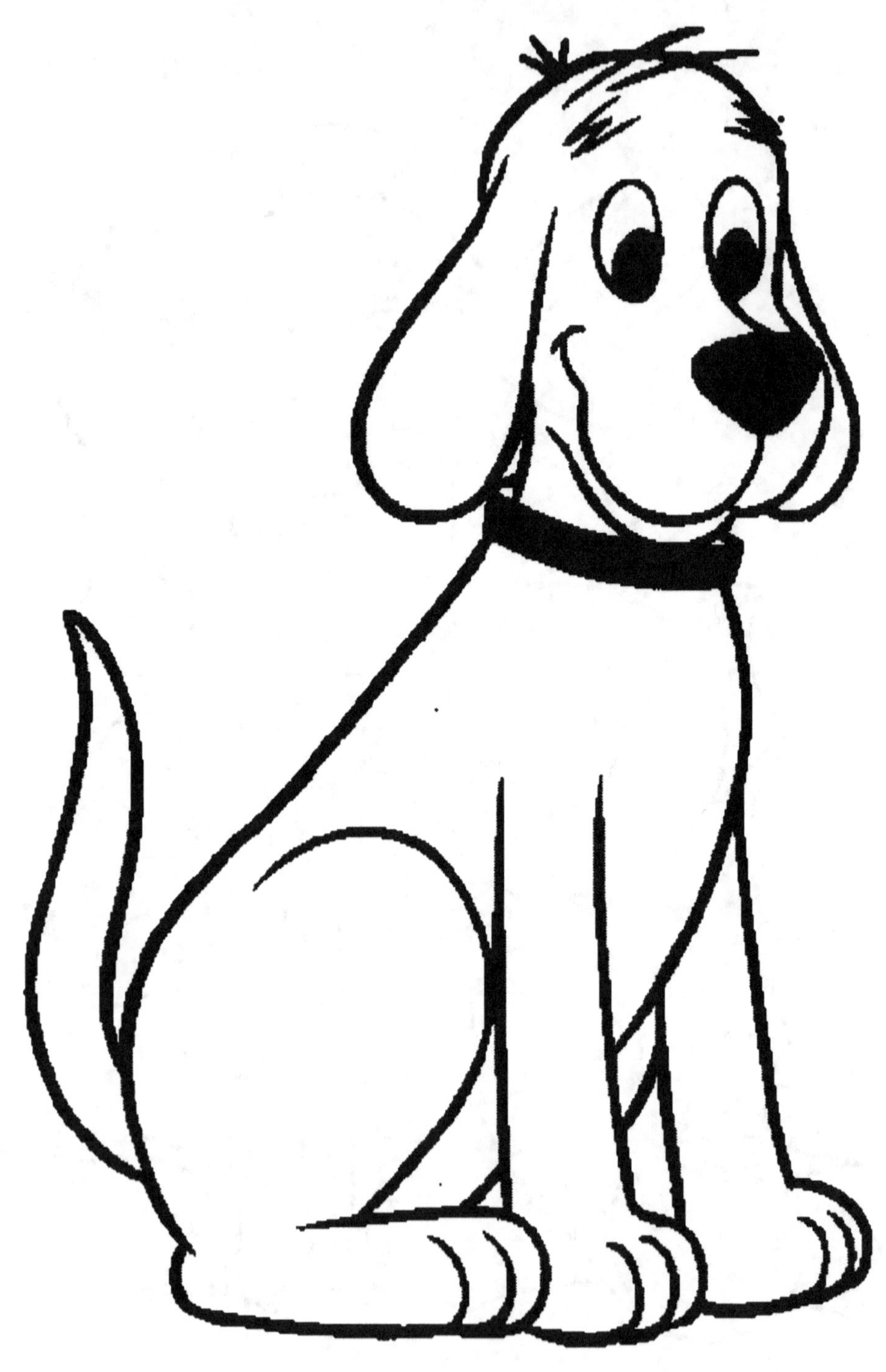

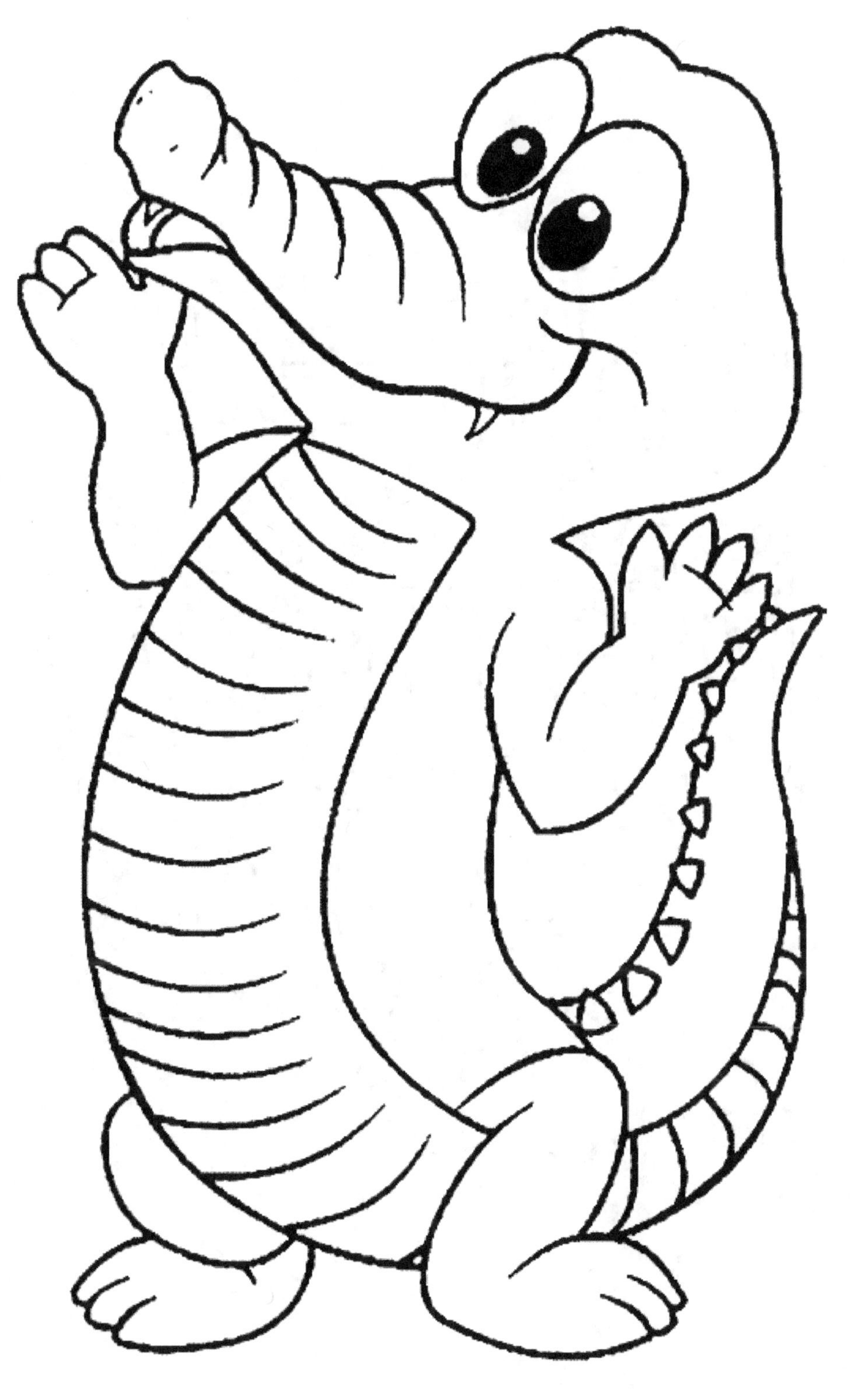

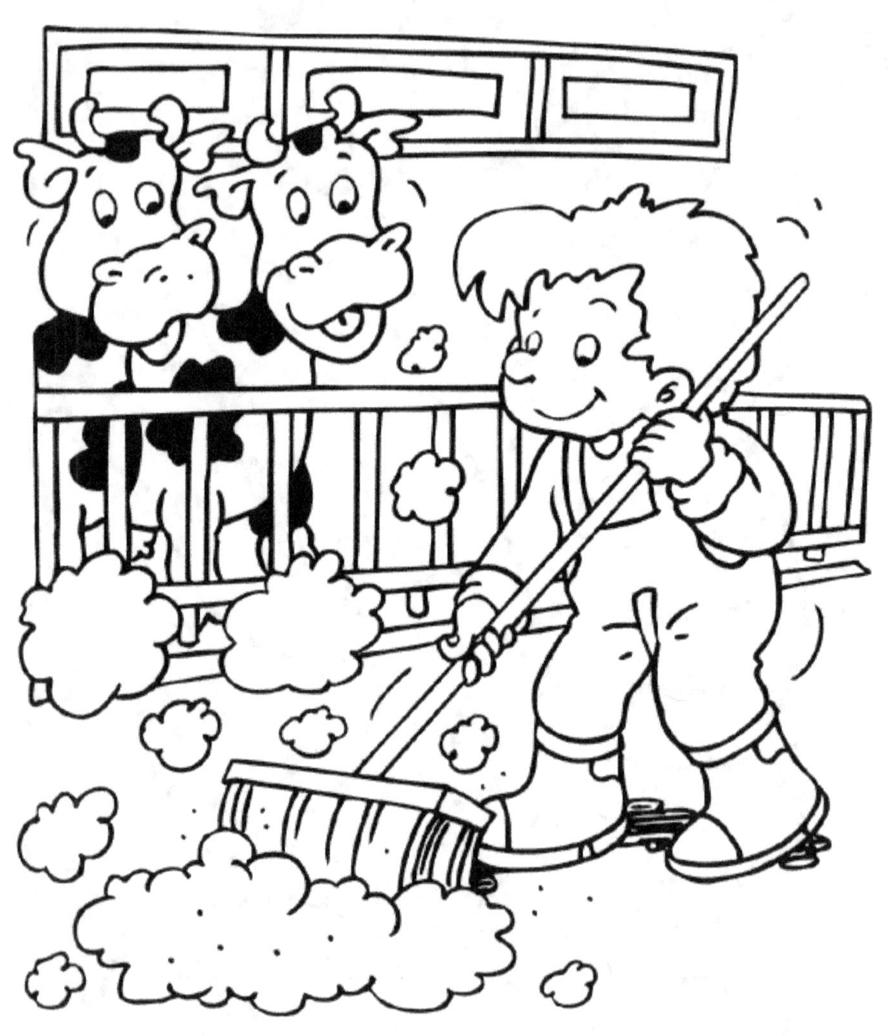

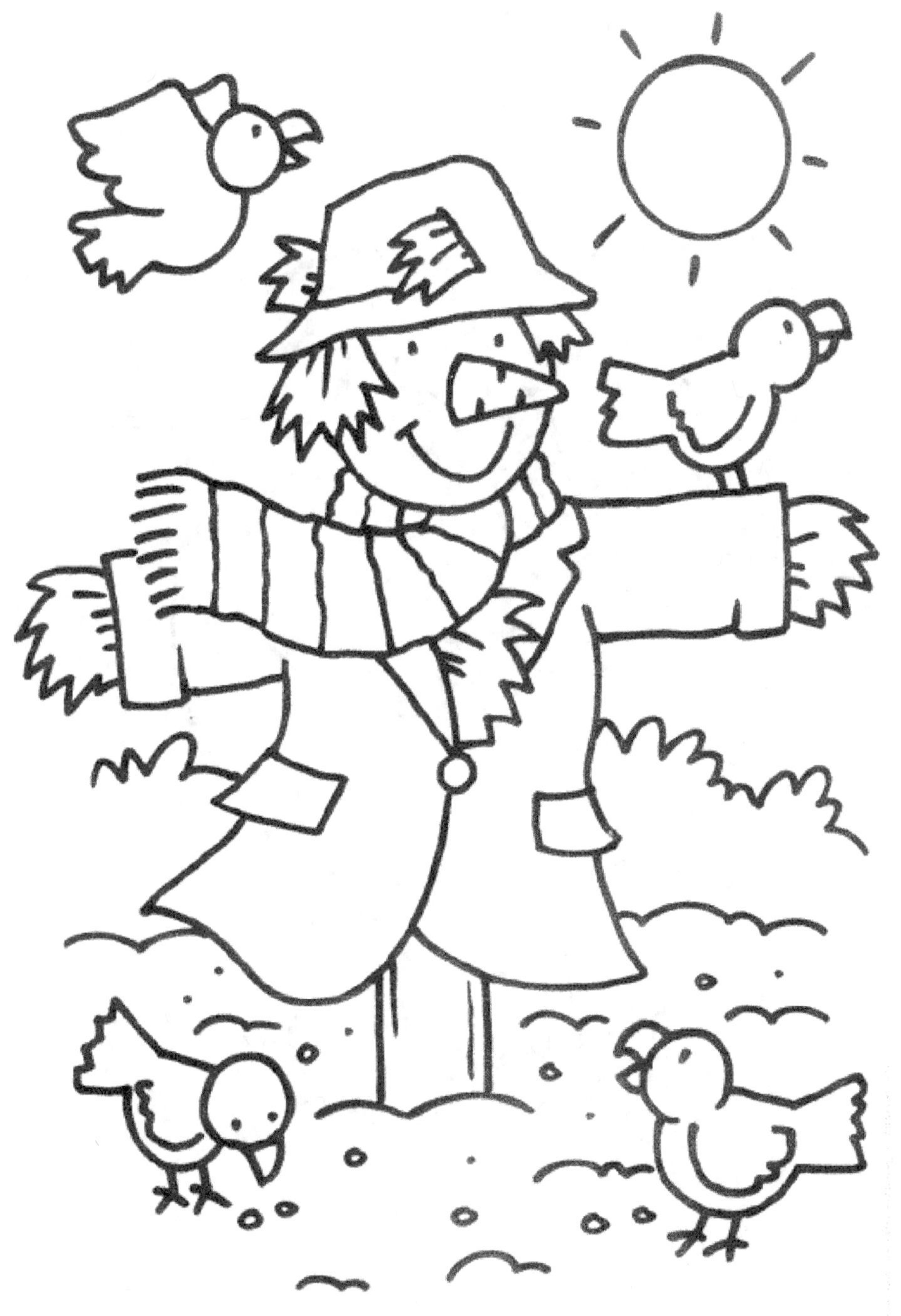

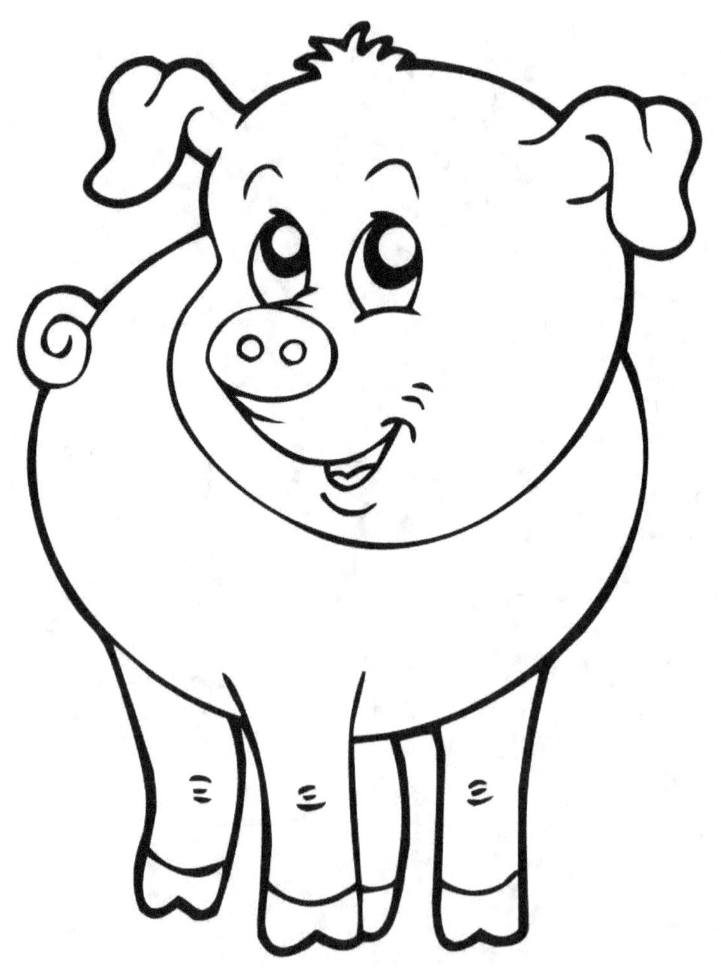

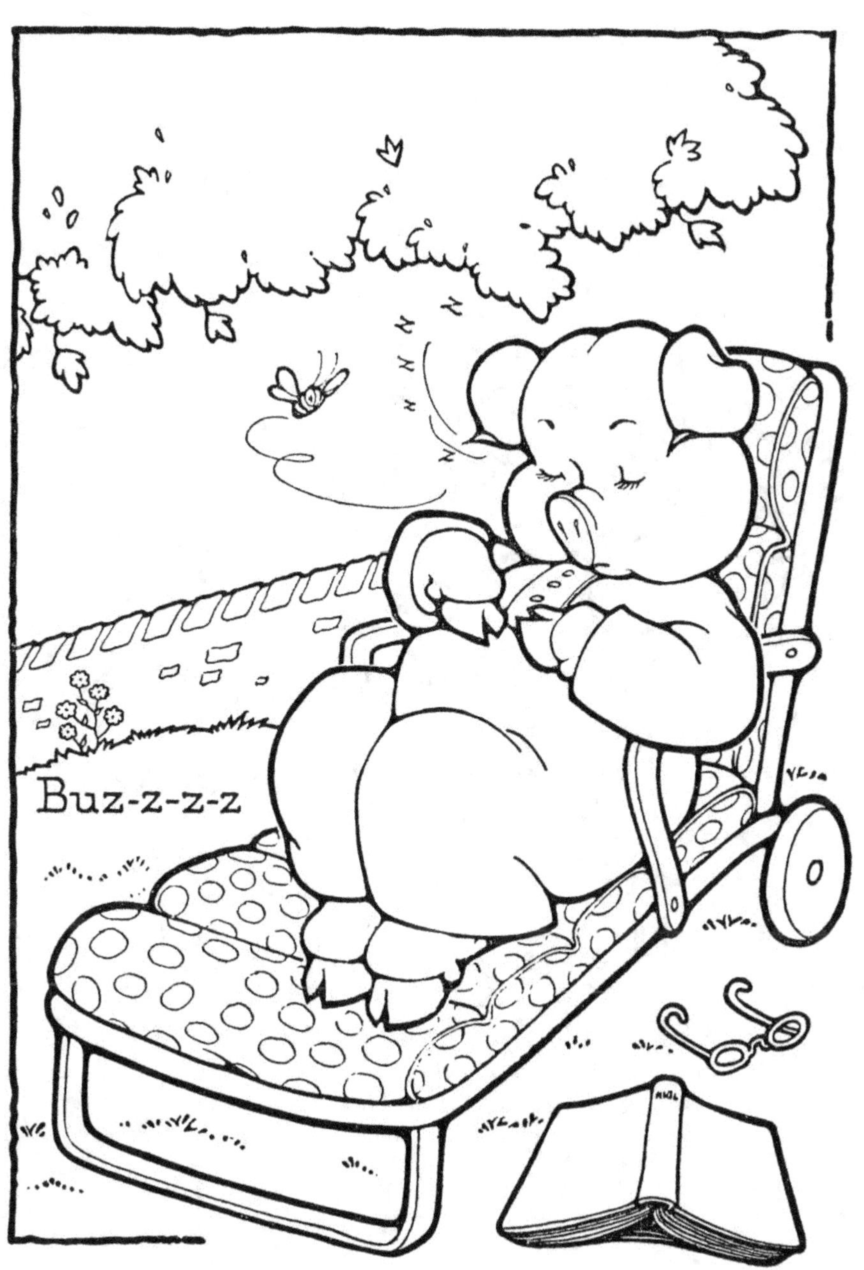
Buz-z-z-z

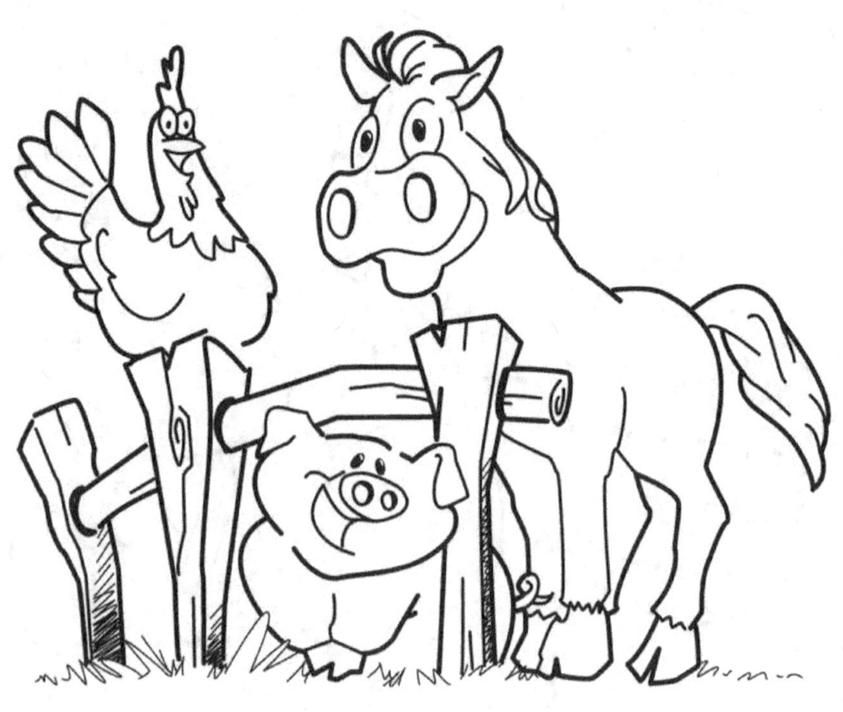

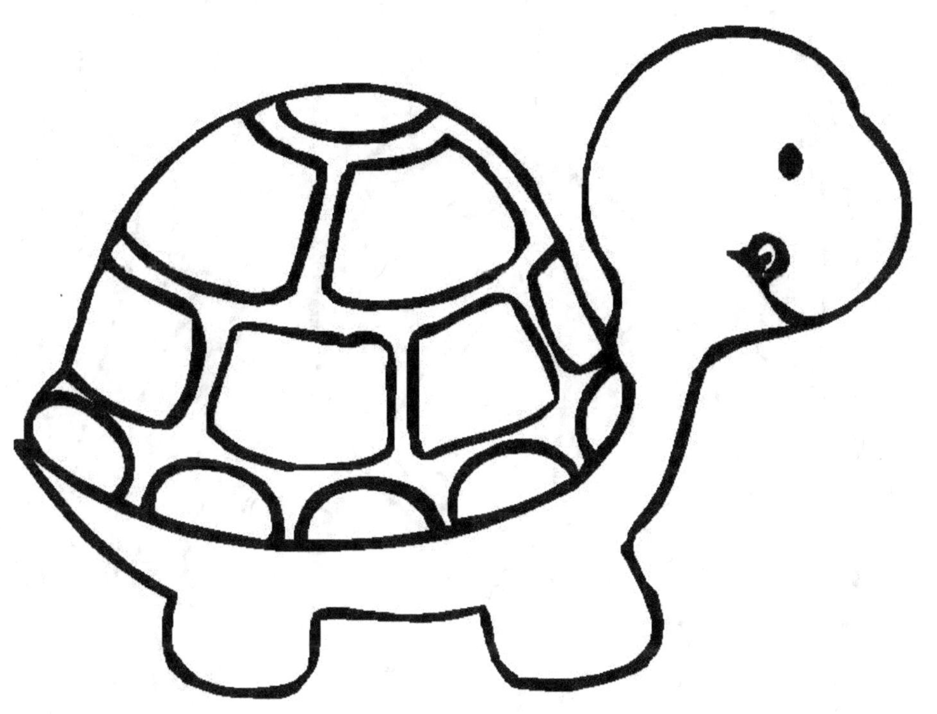

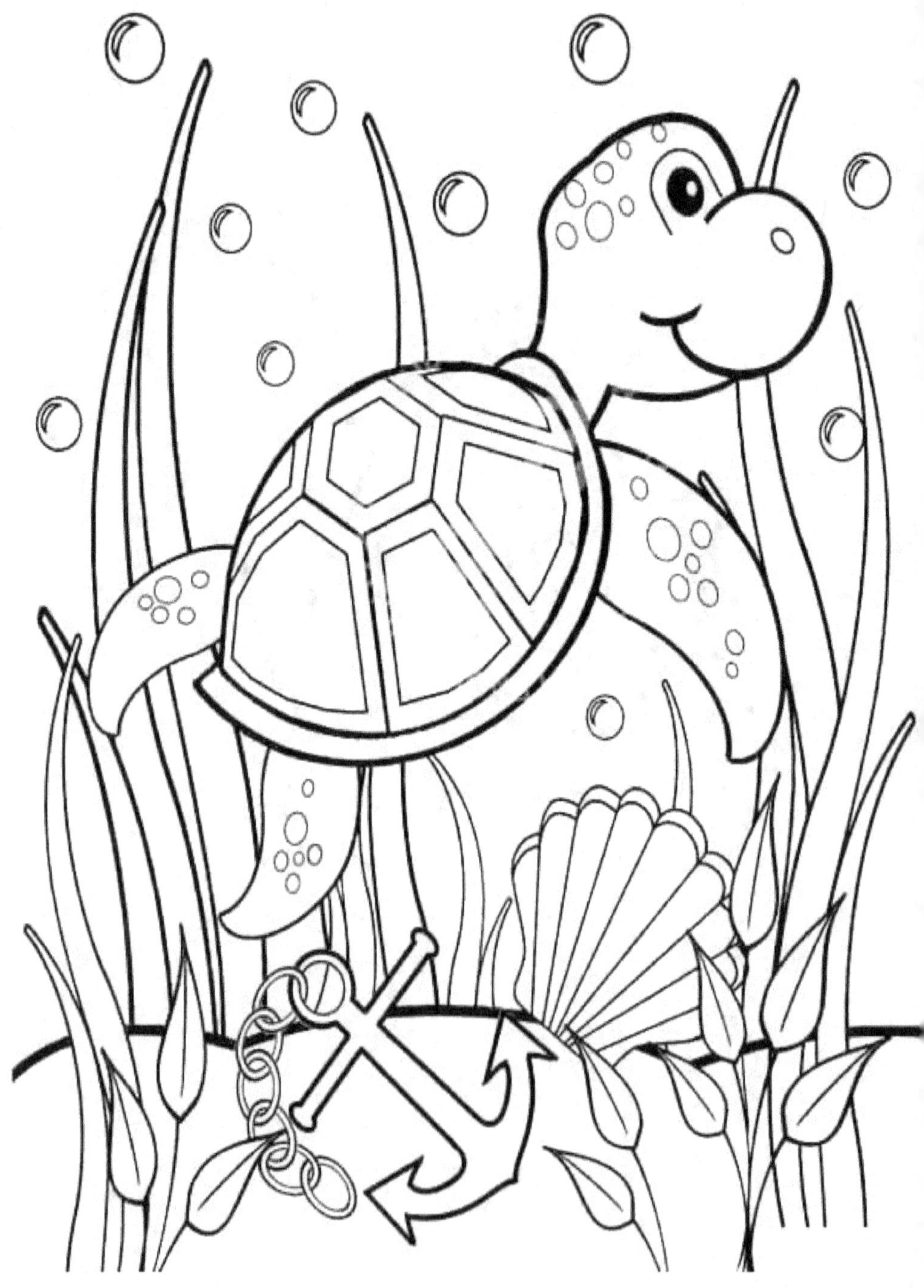

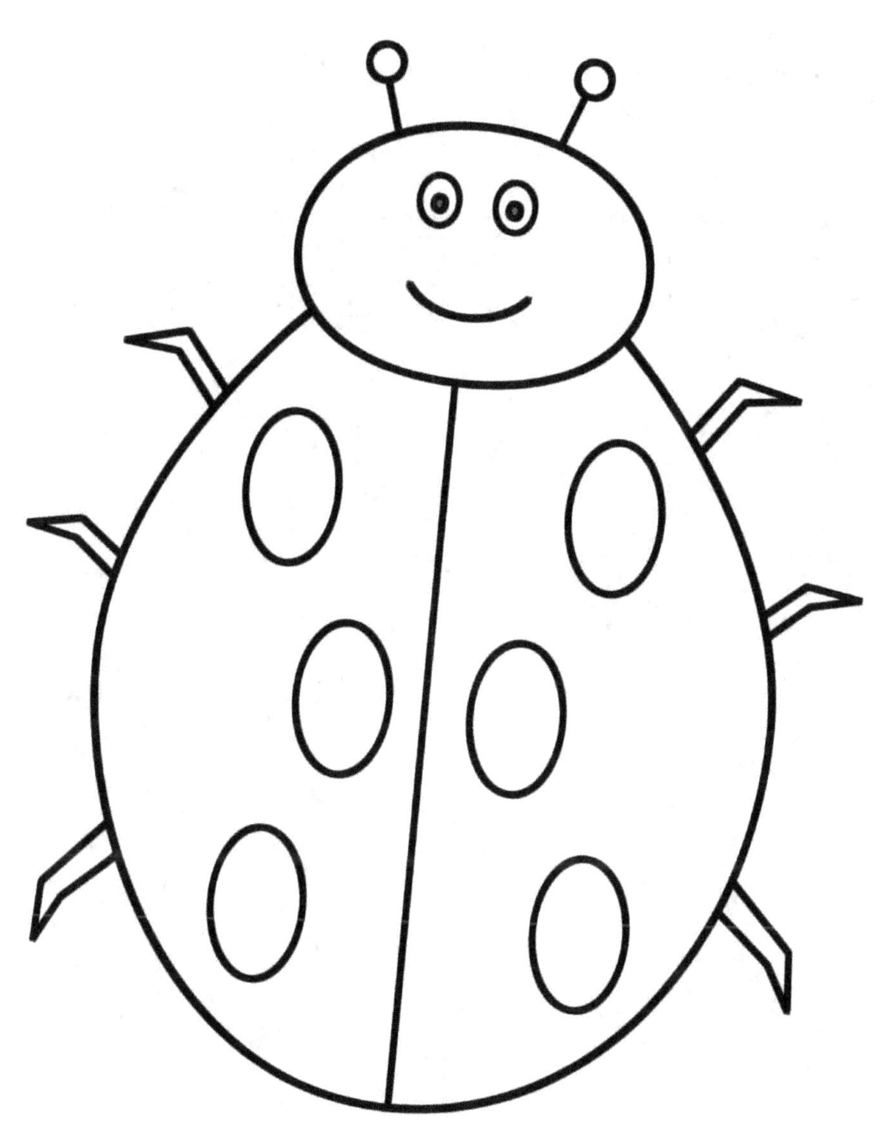

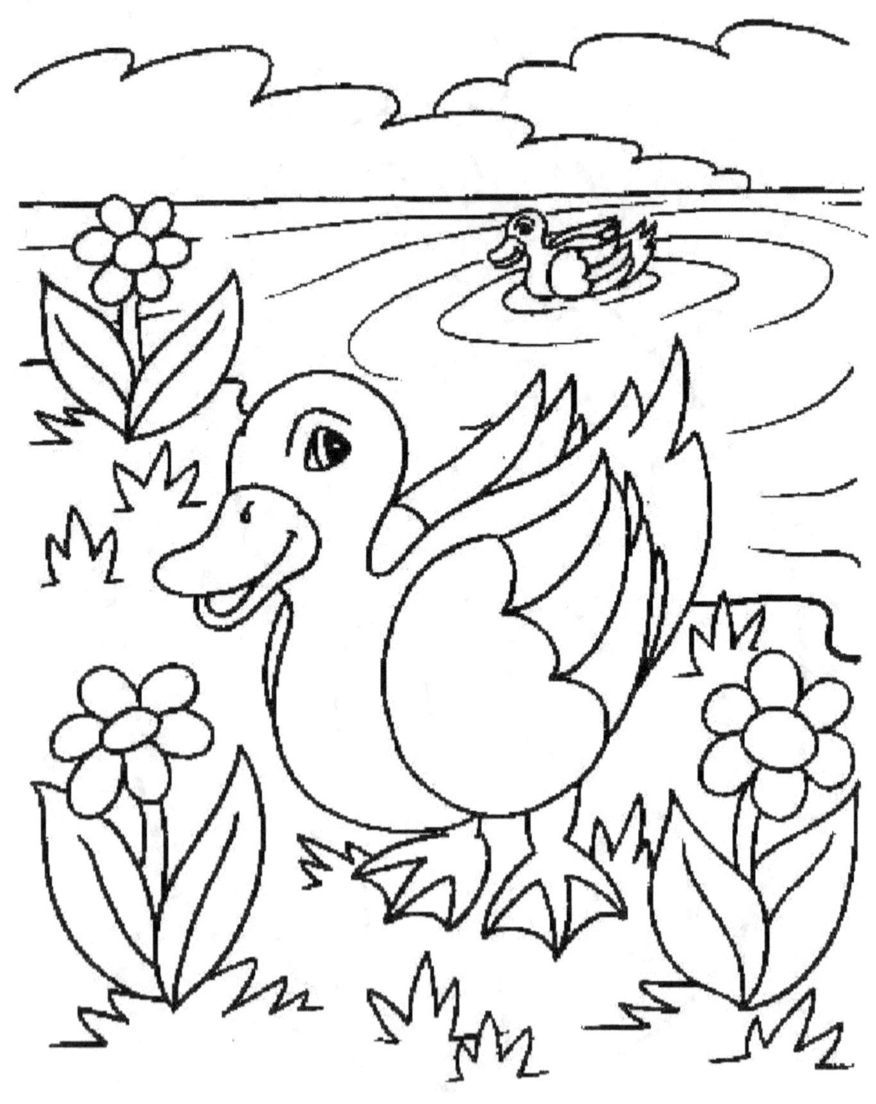

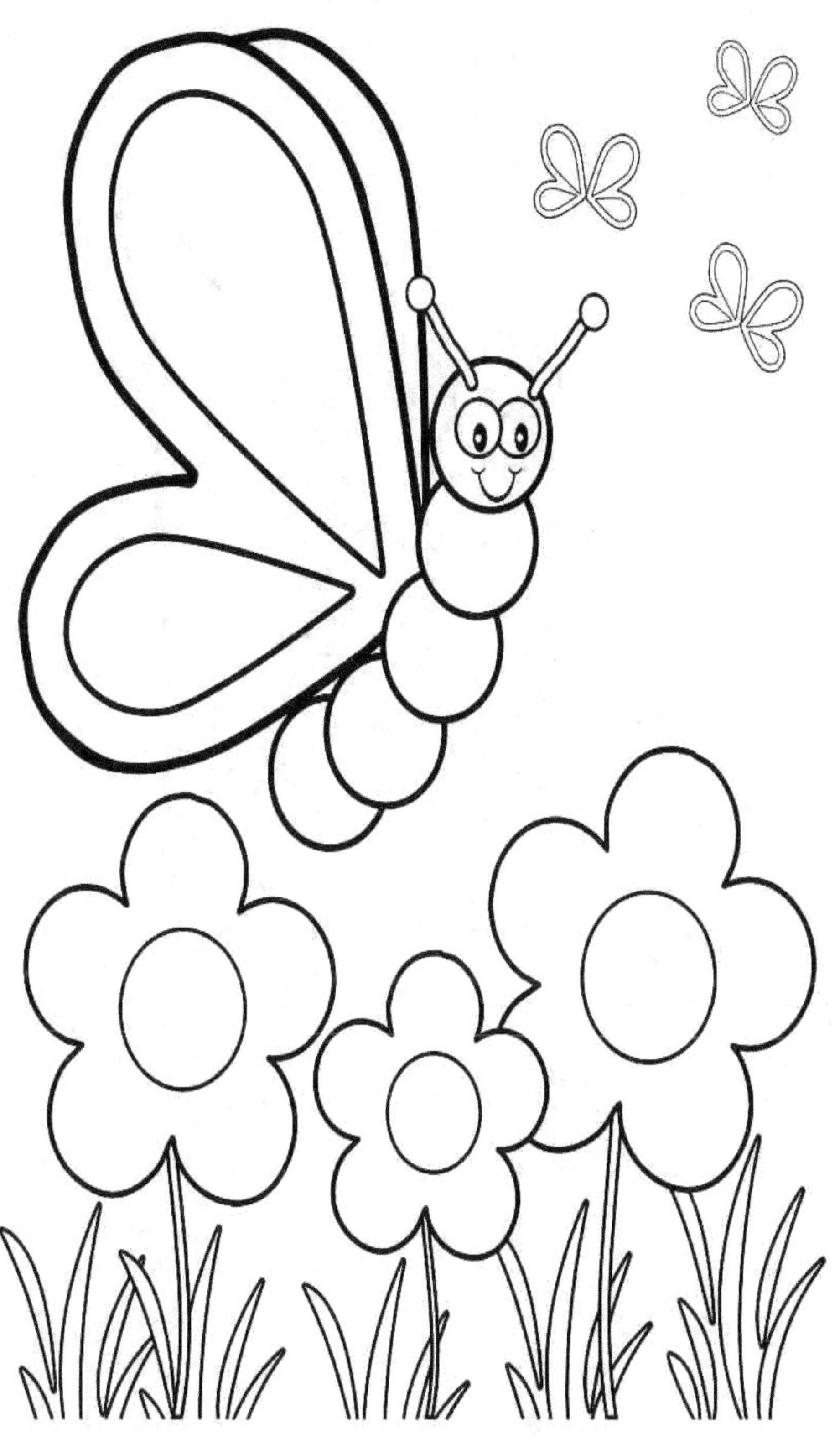

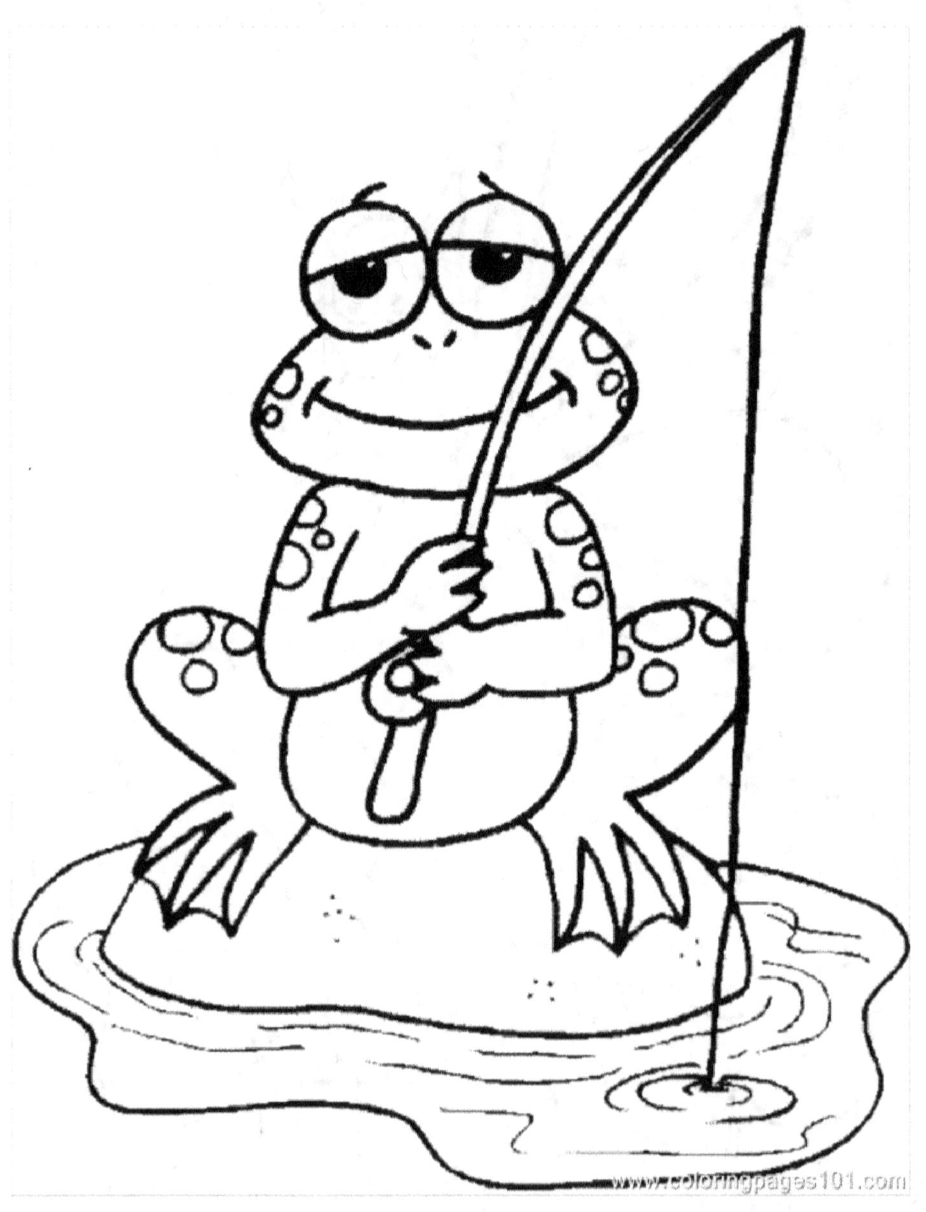
www.coloringpages101.com

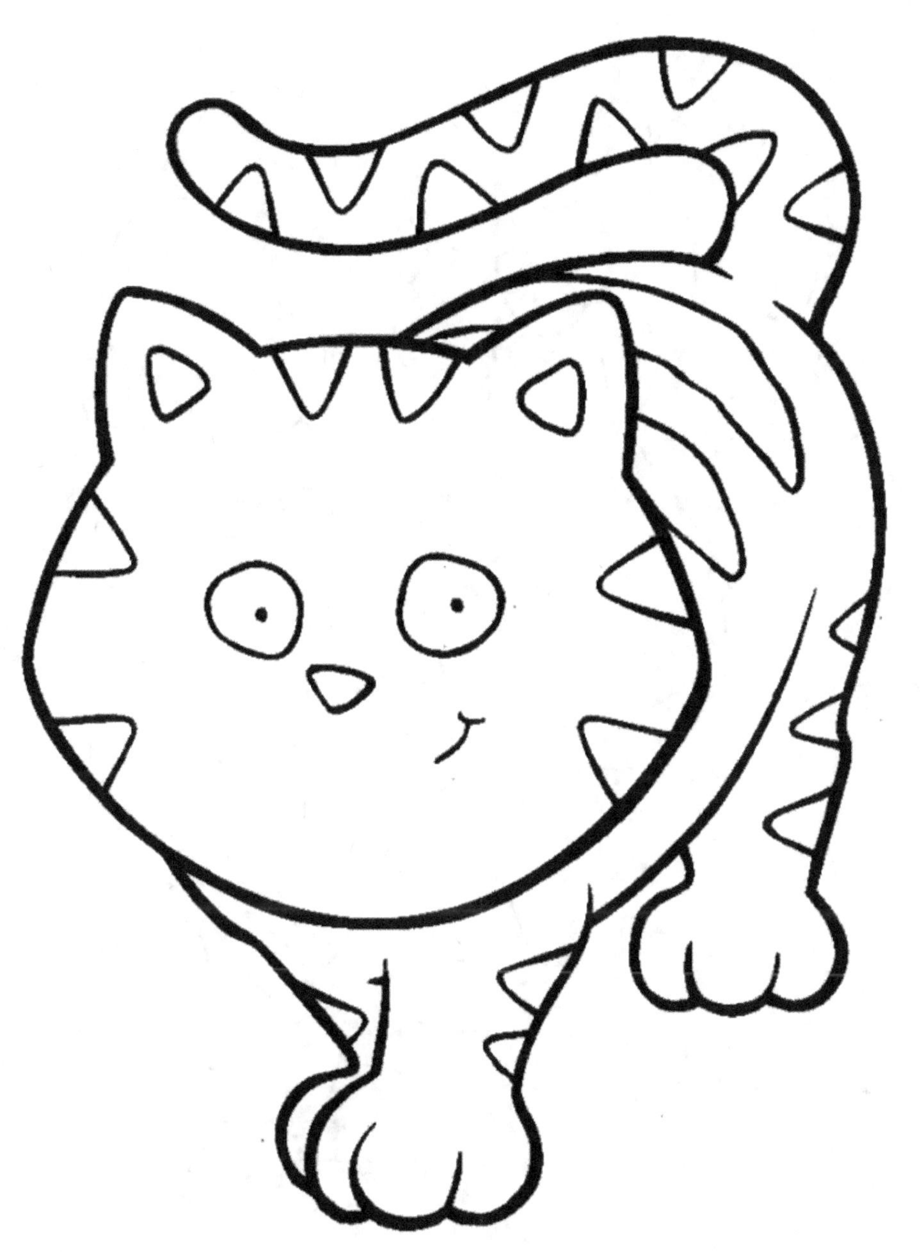

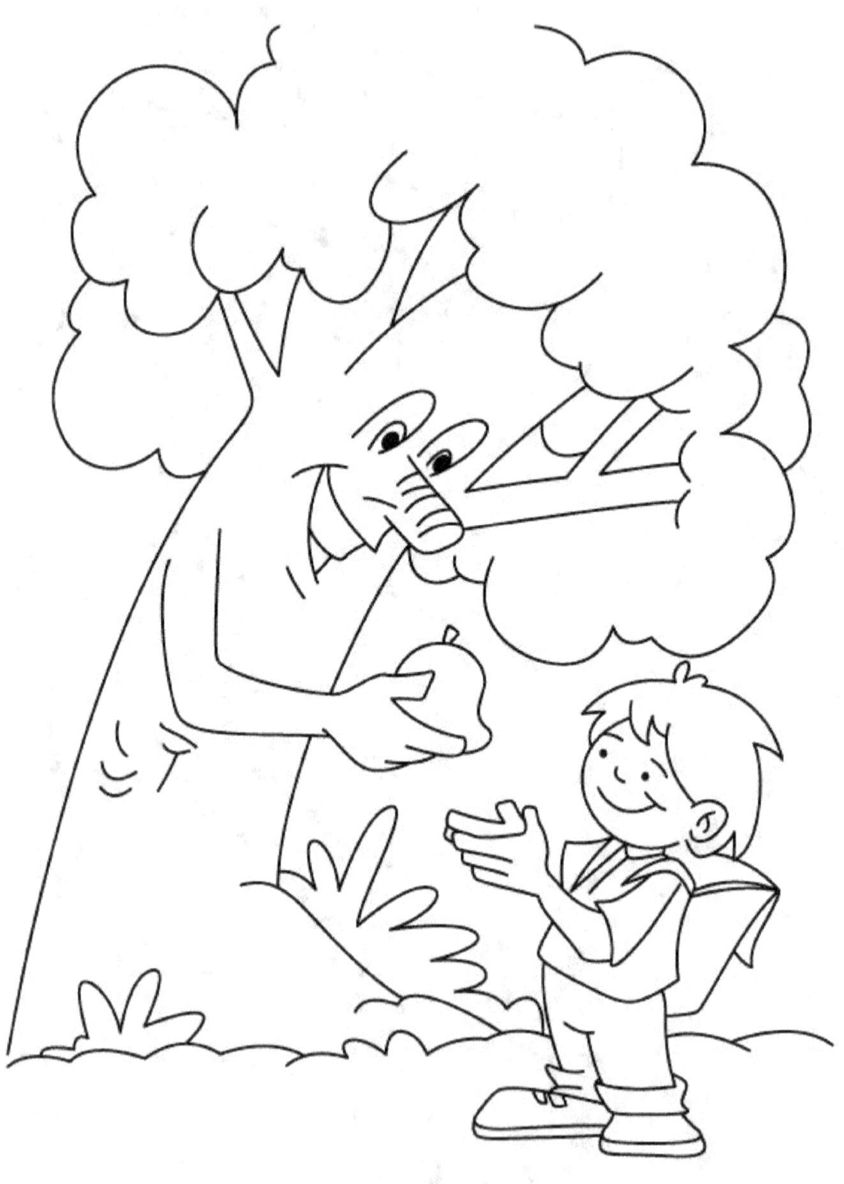

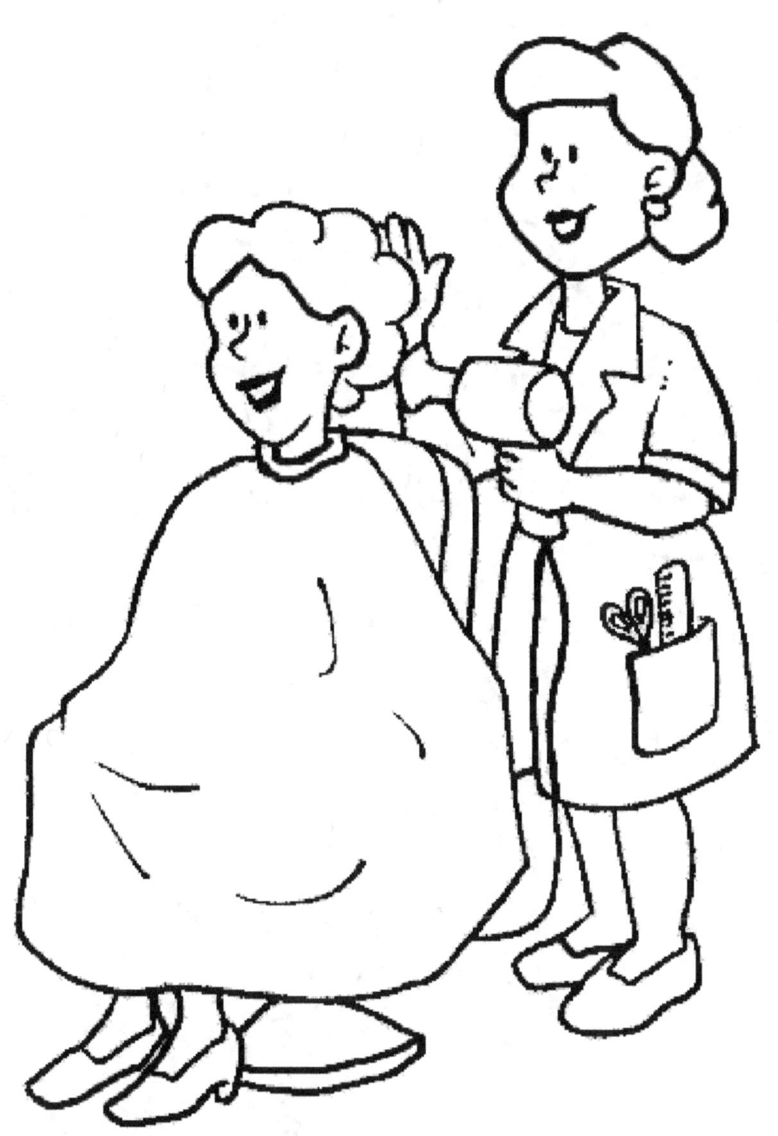

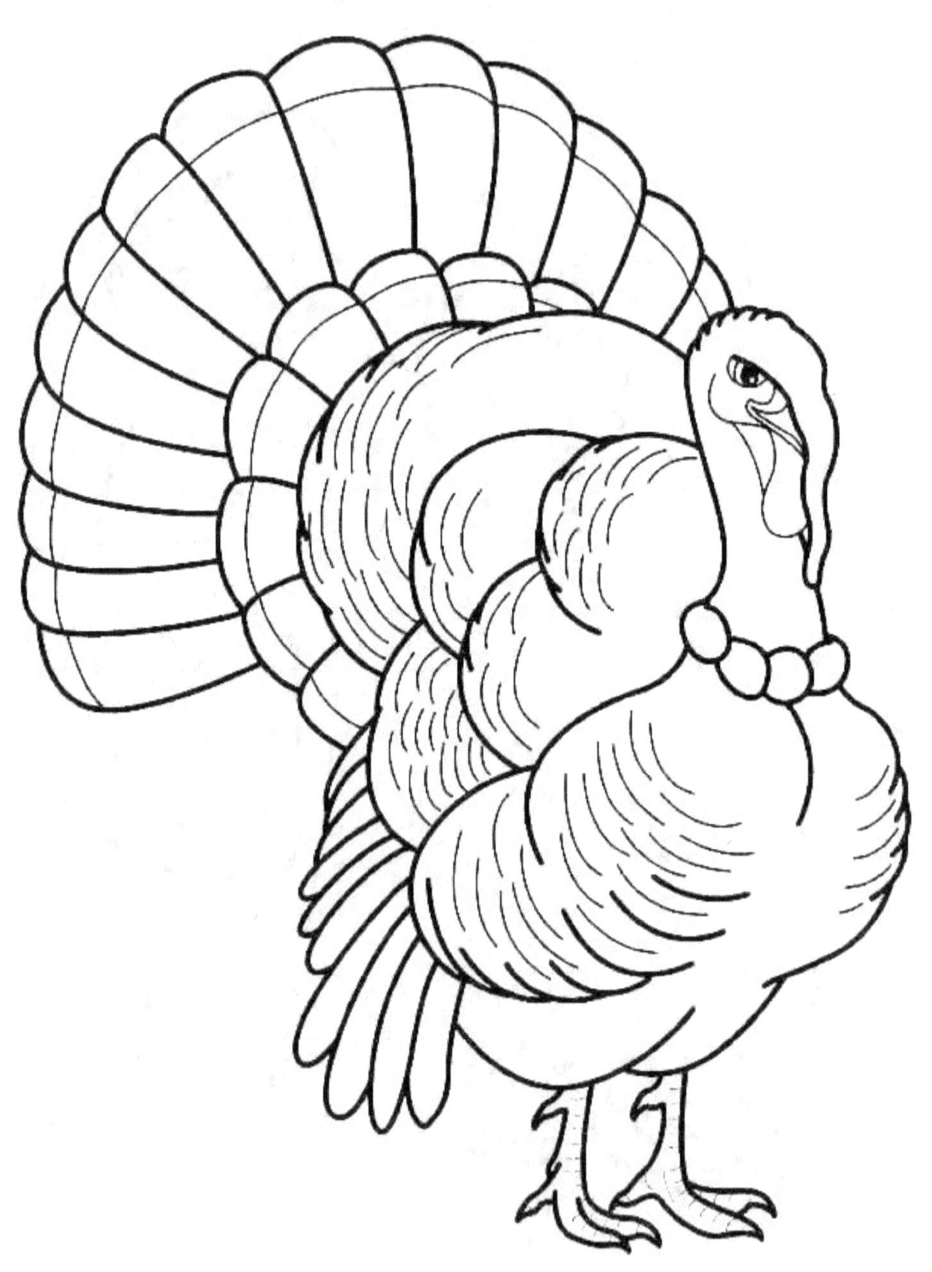

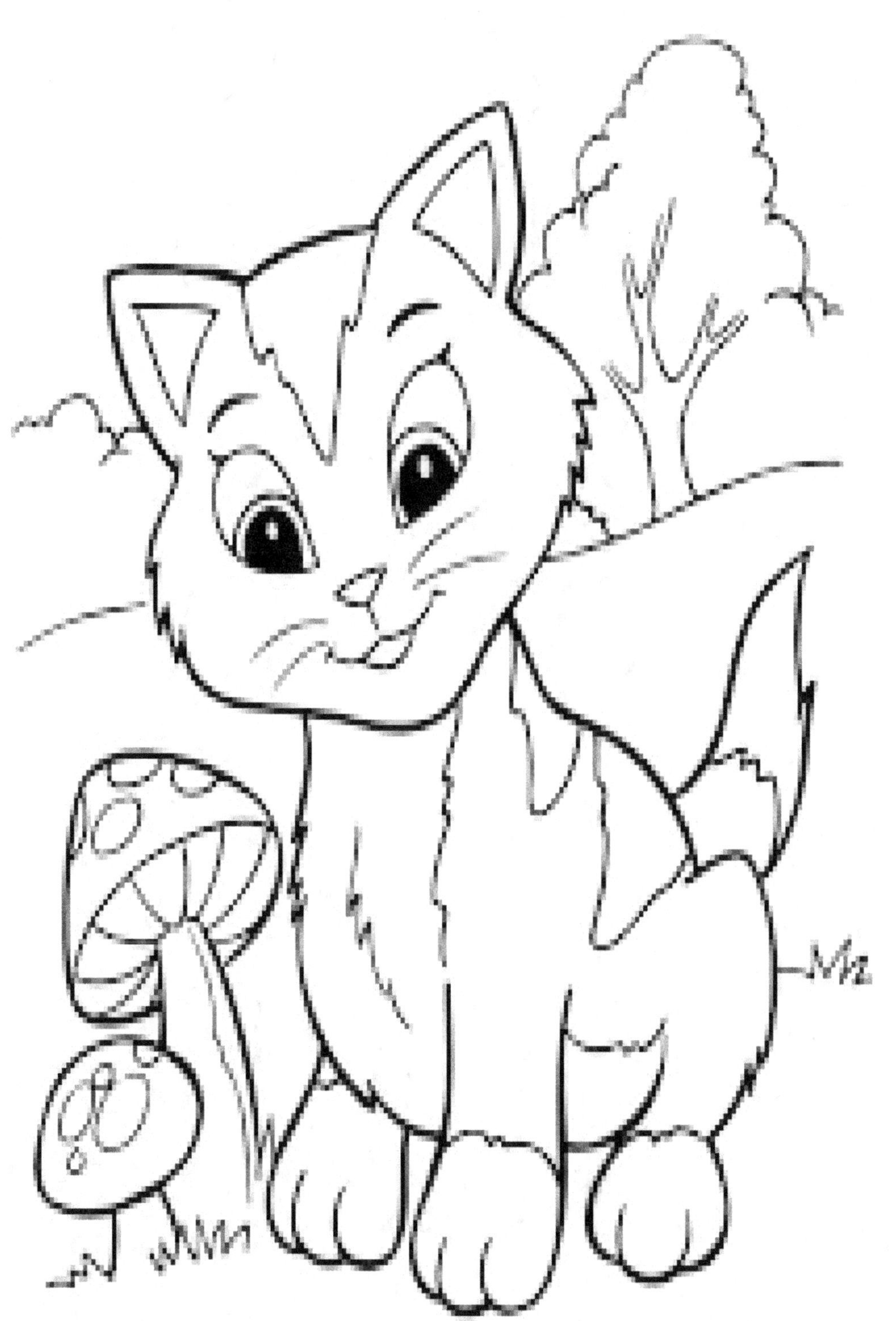

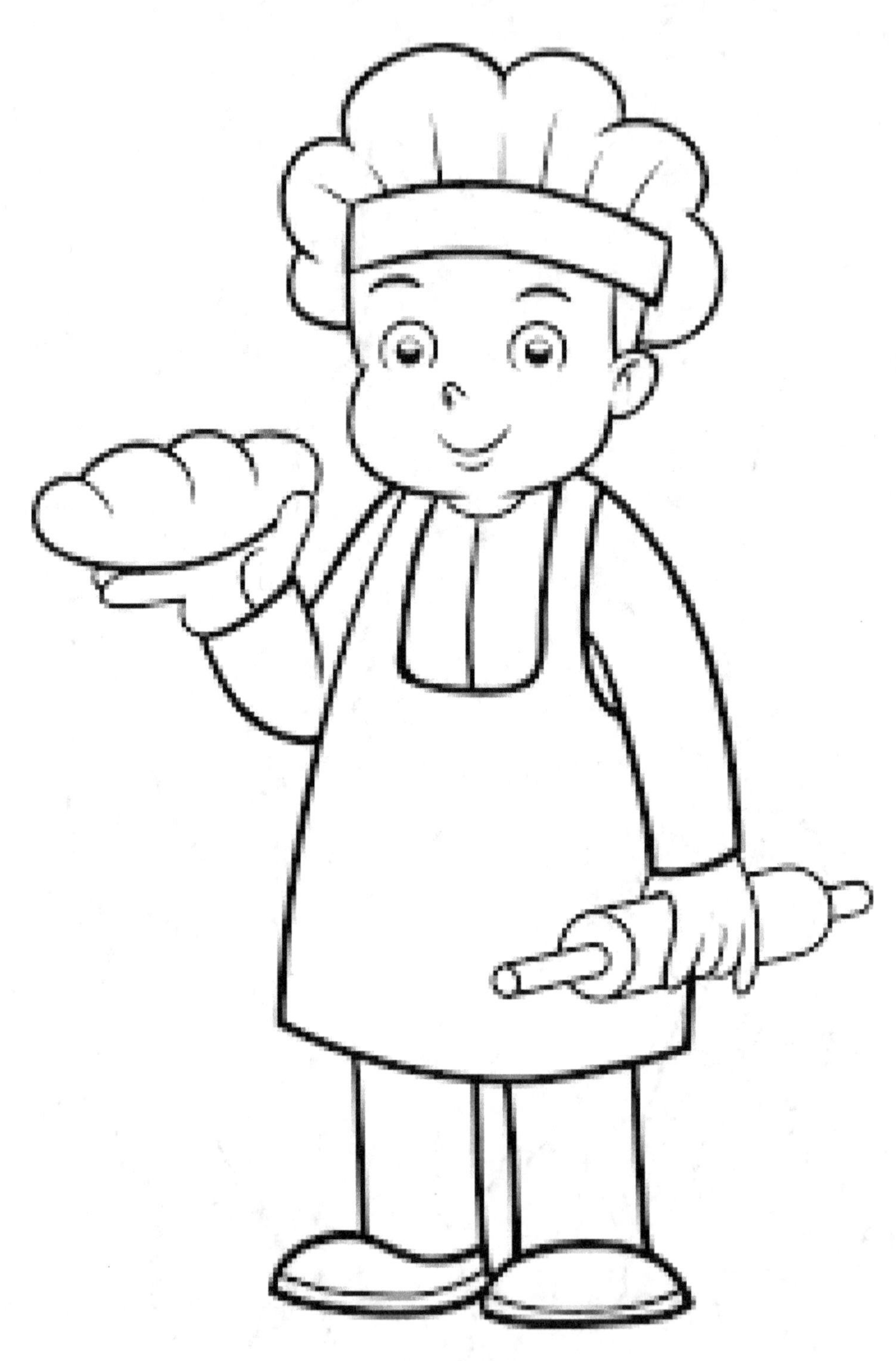

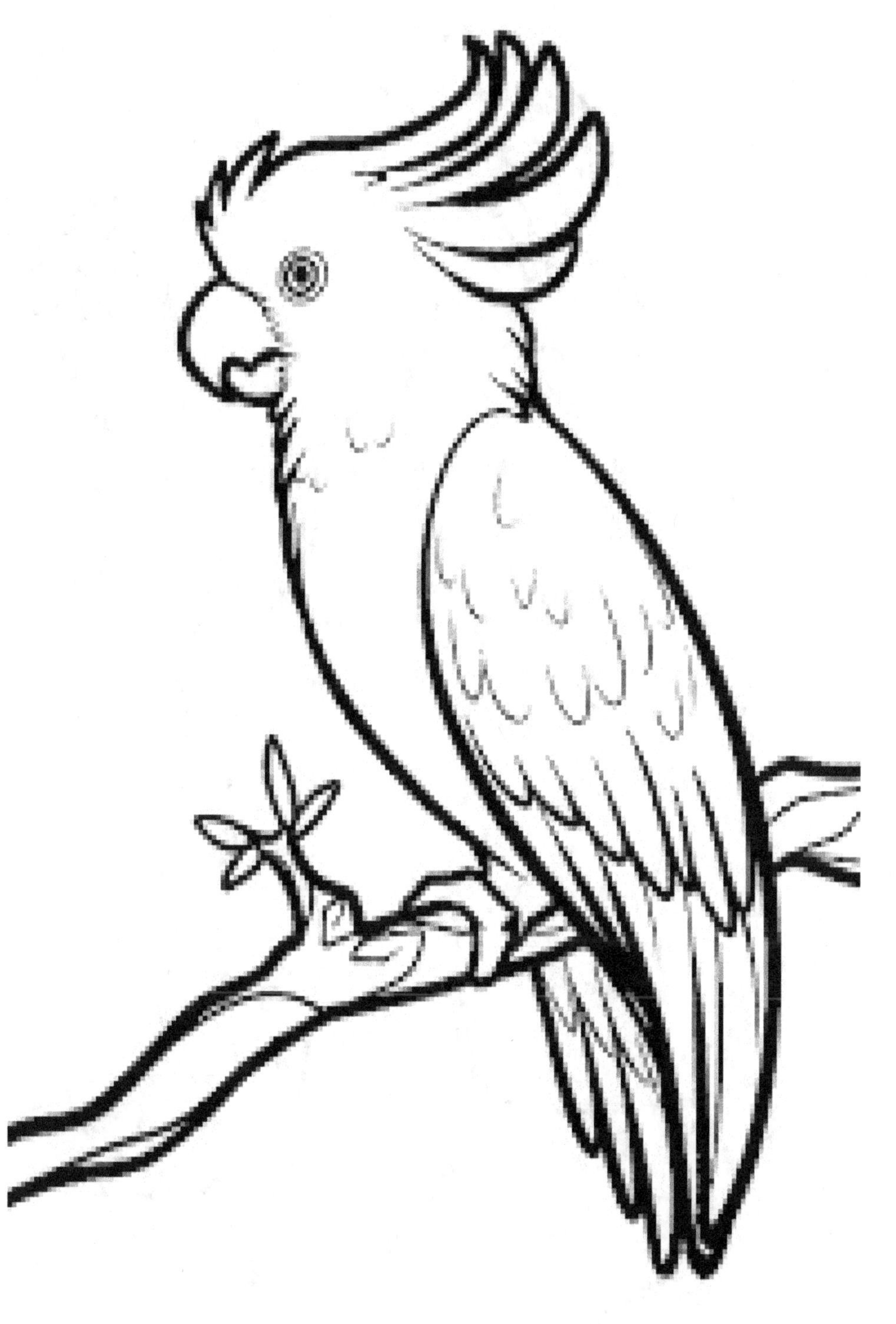

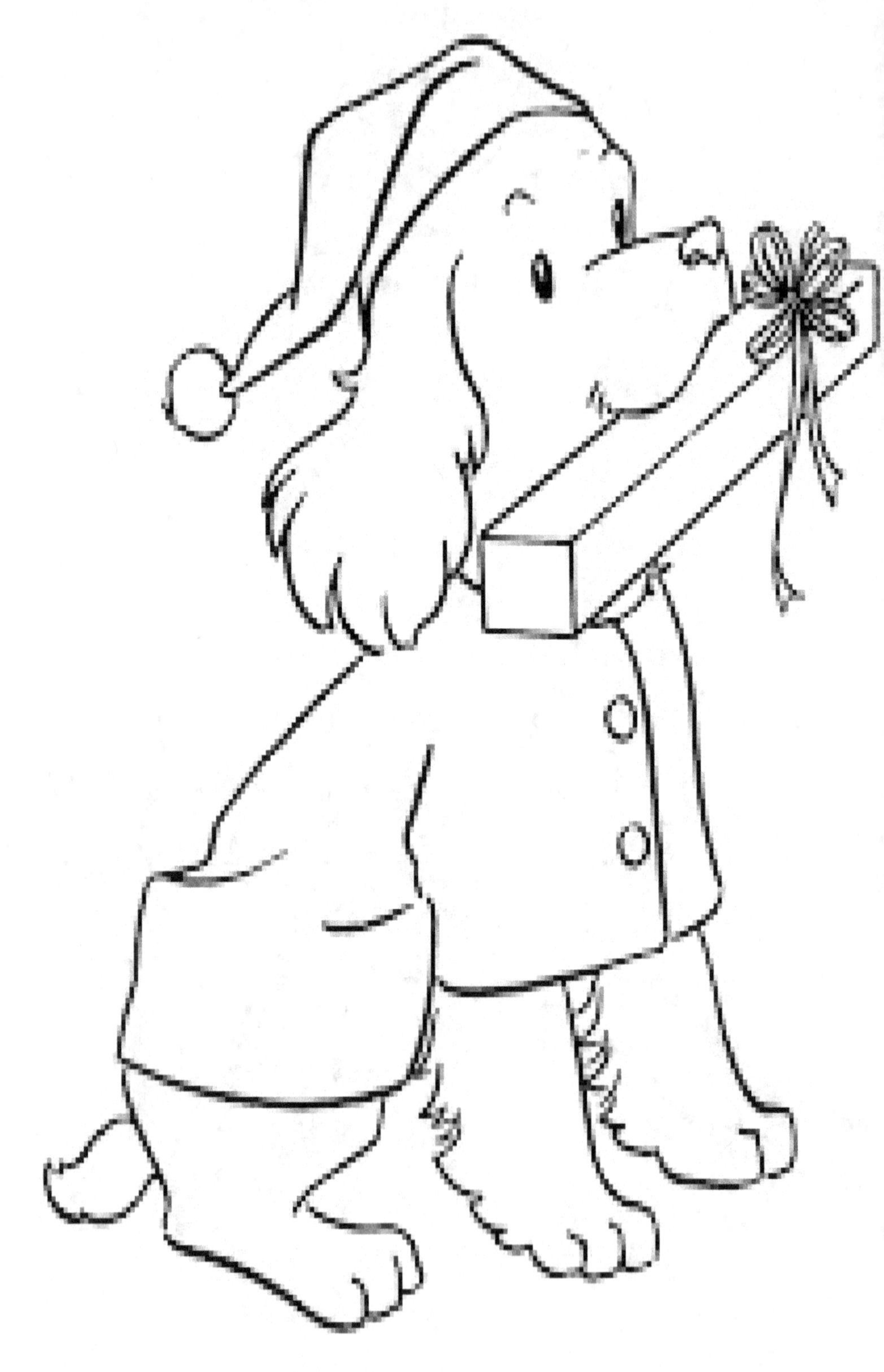

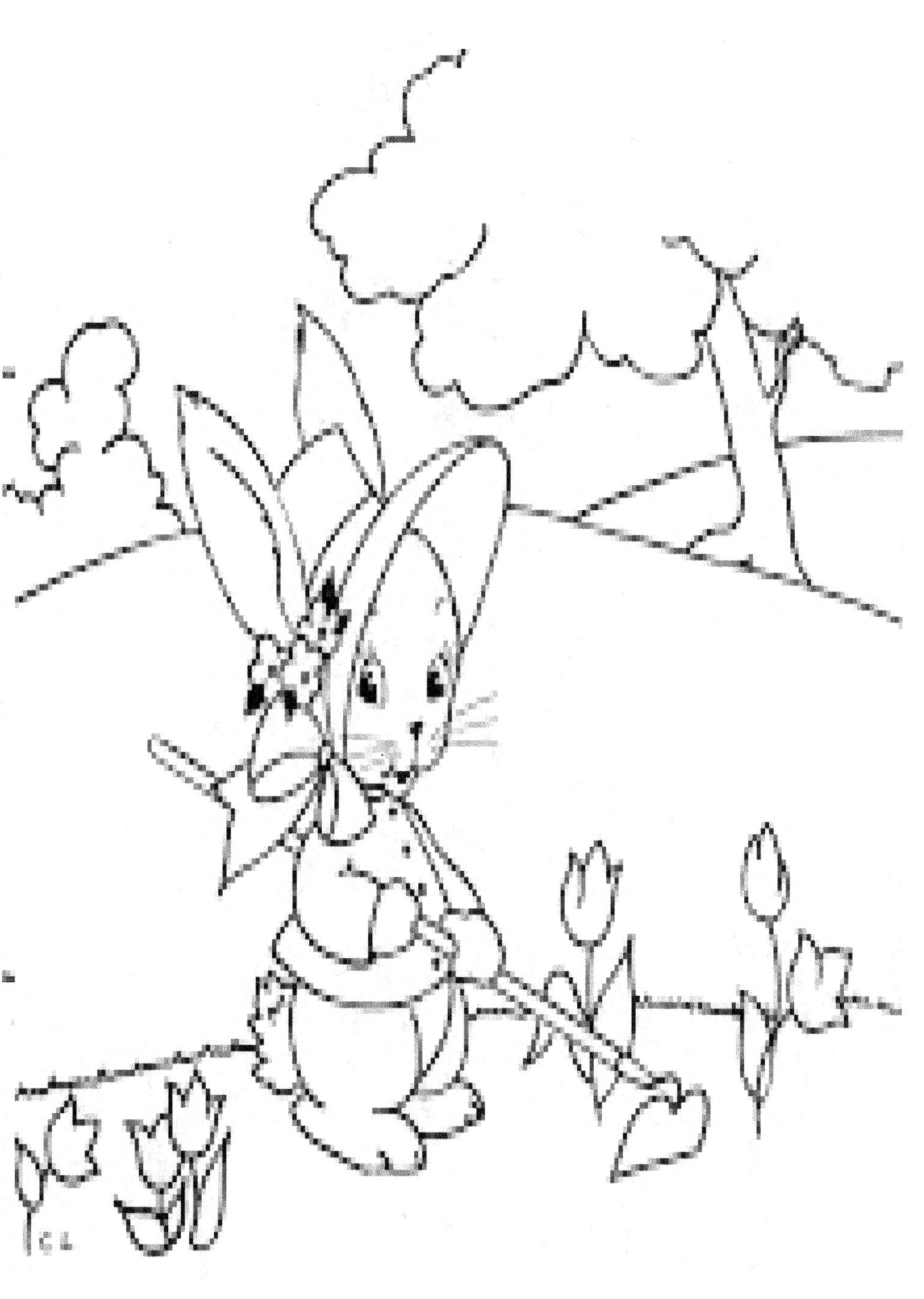

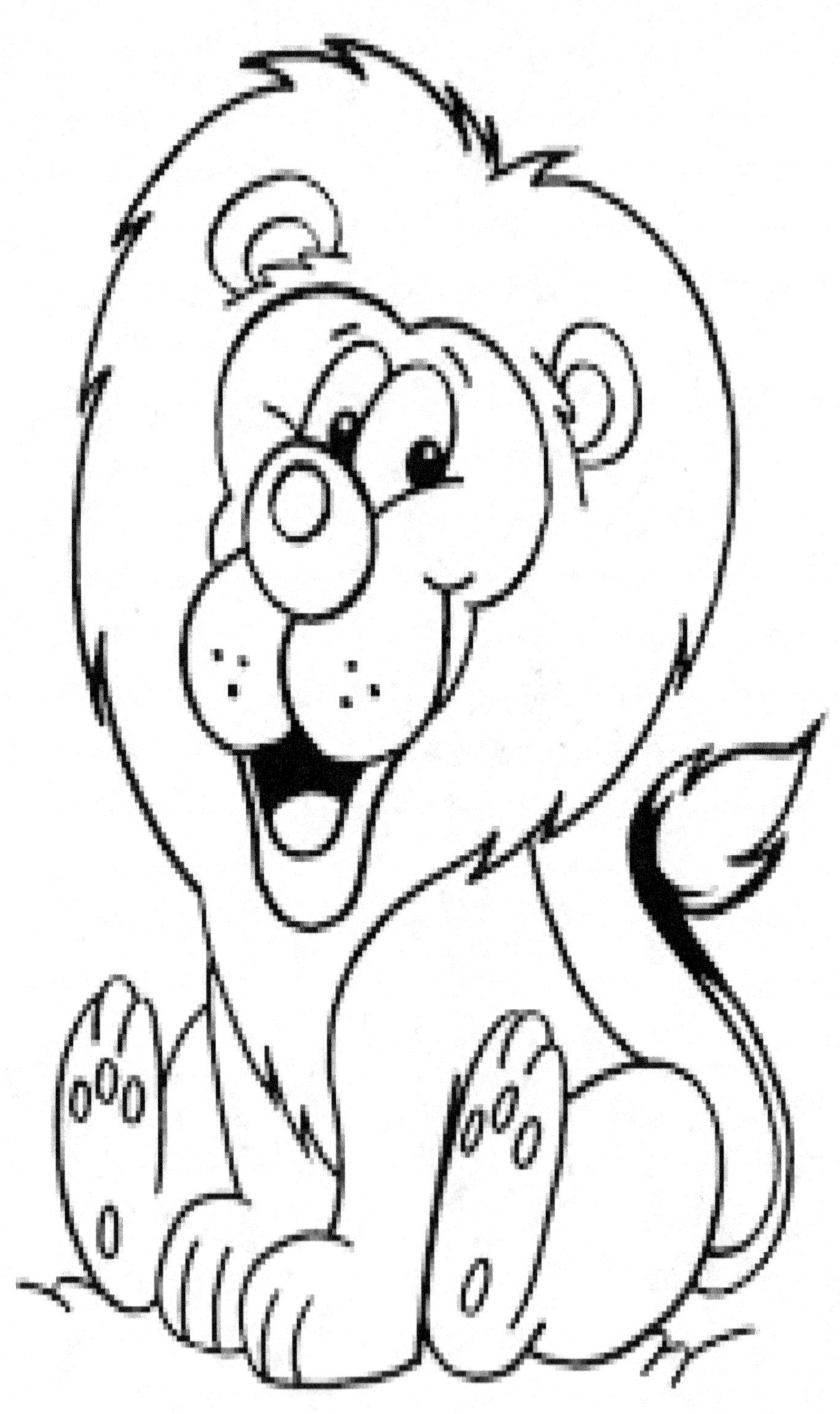

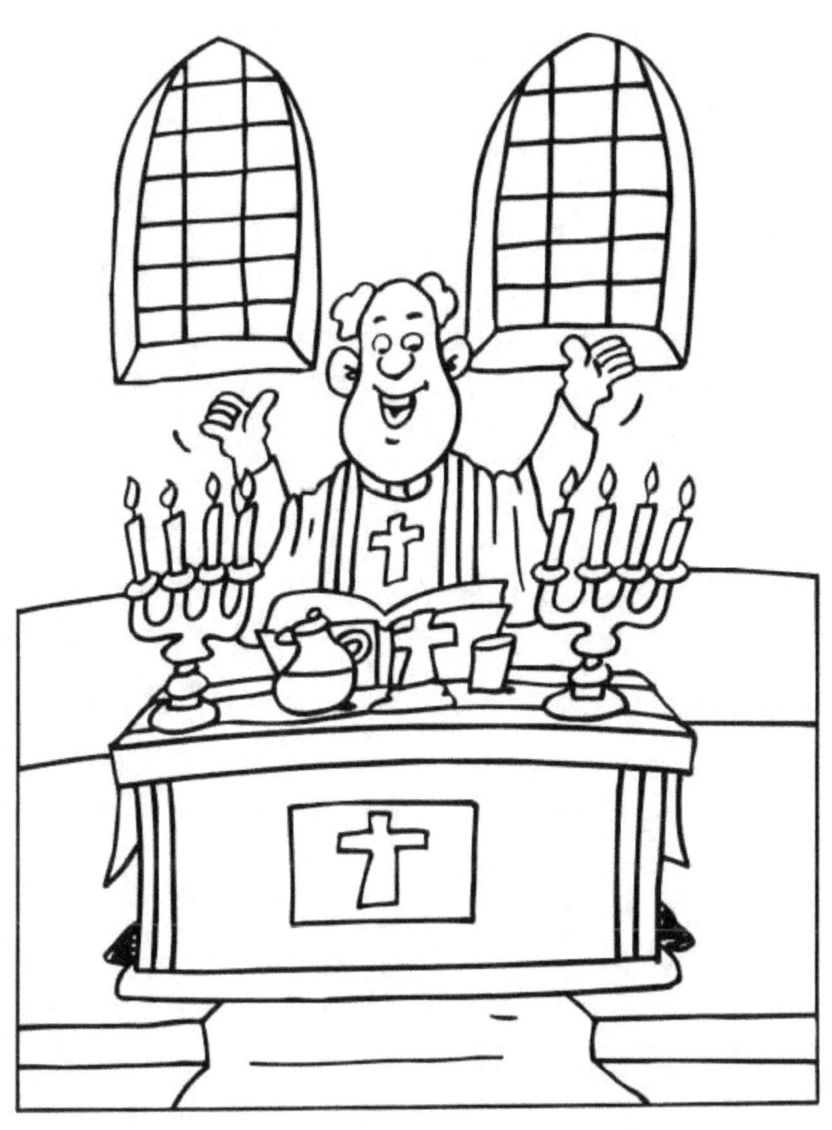

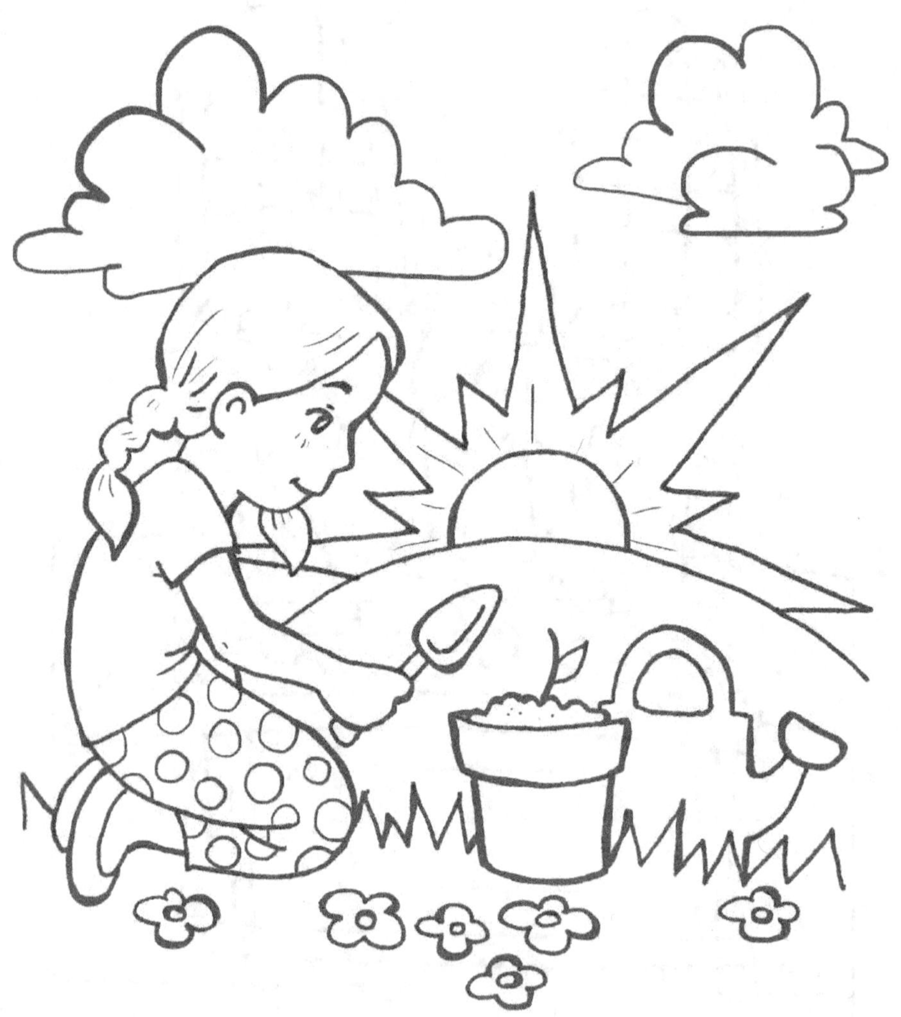

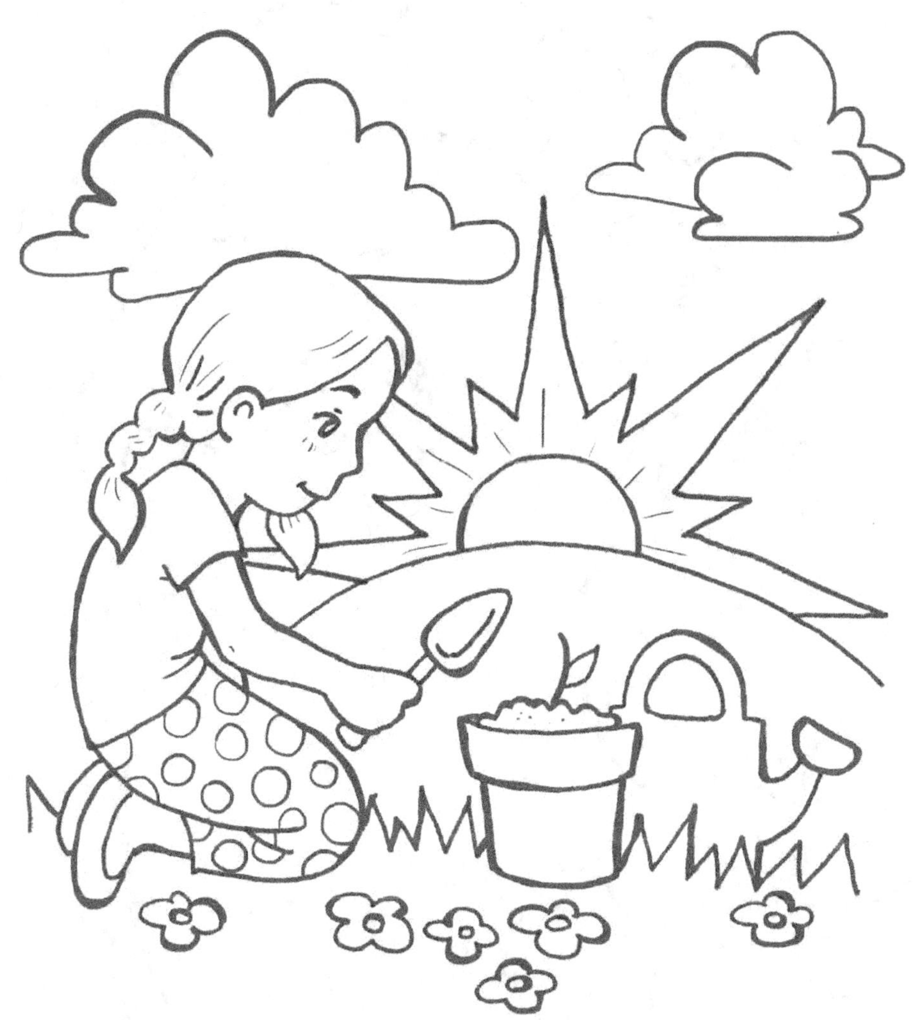

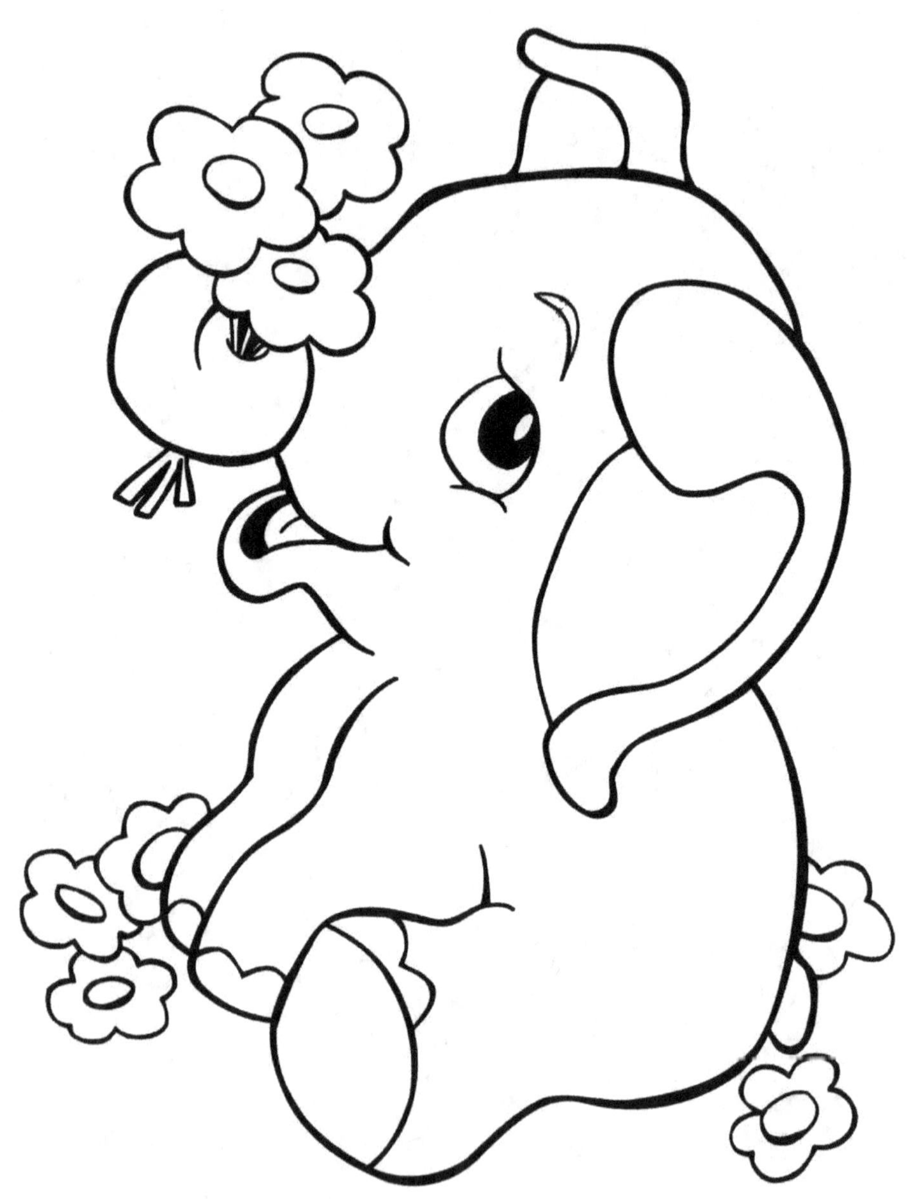

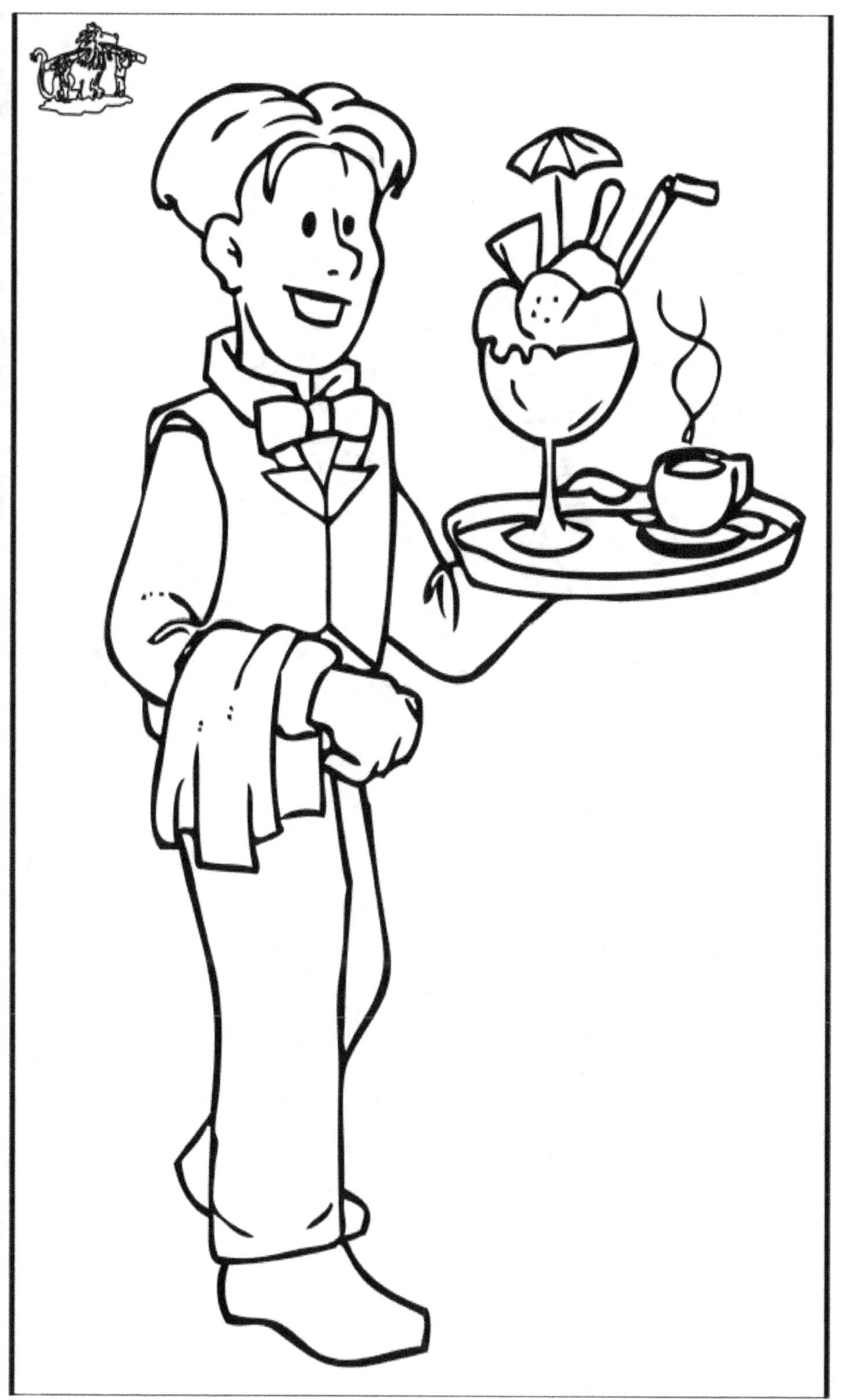

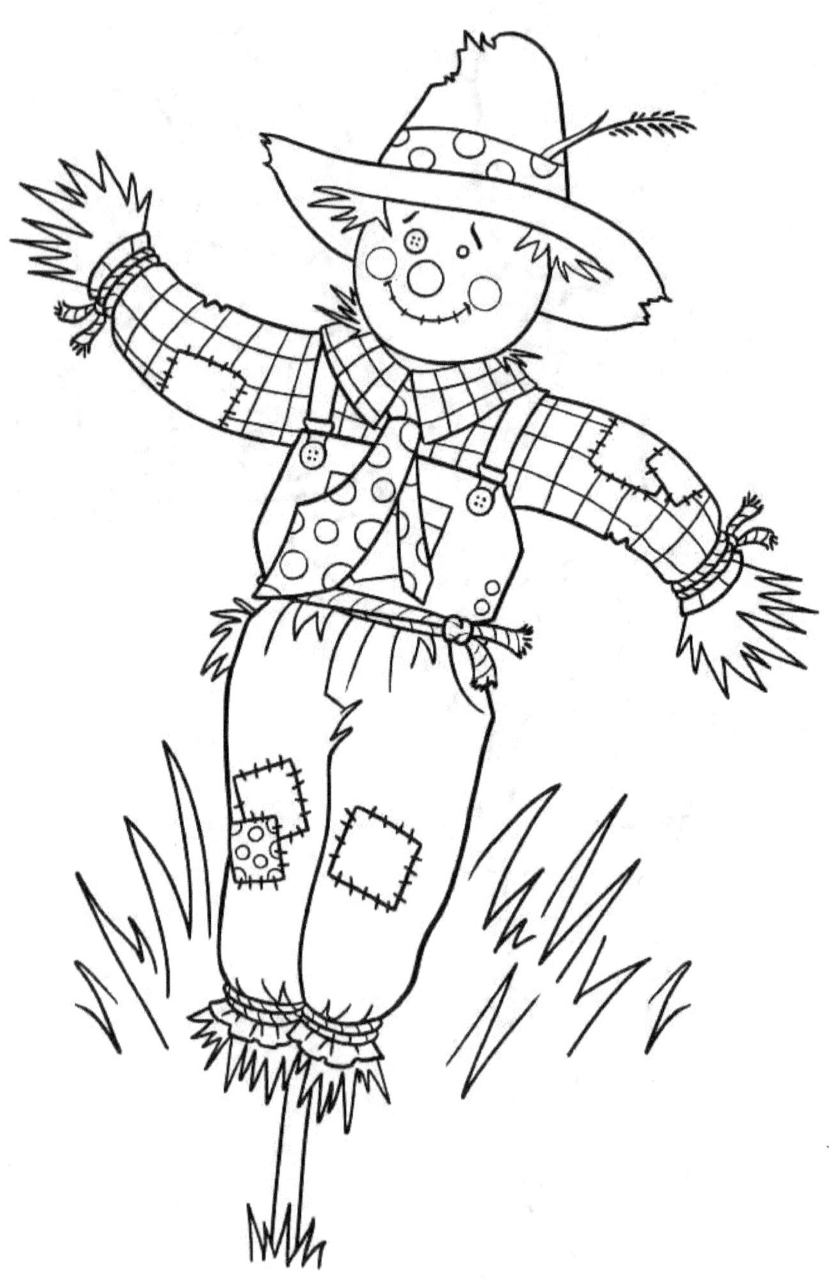

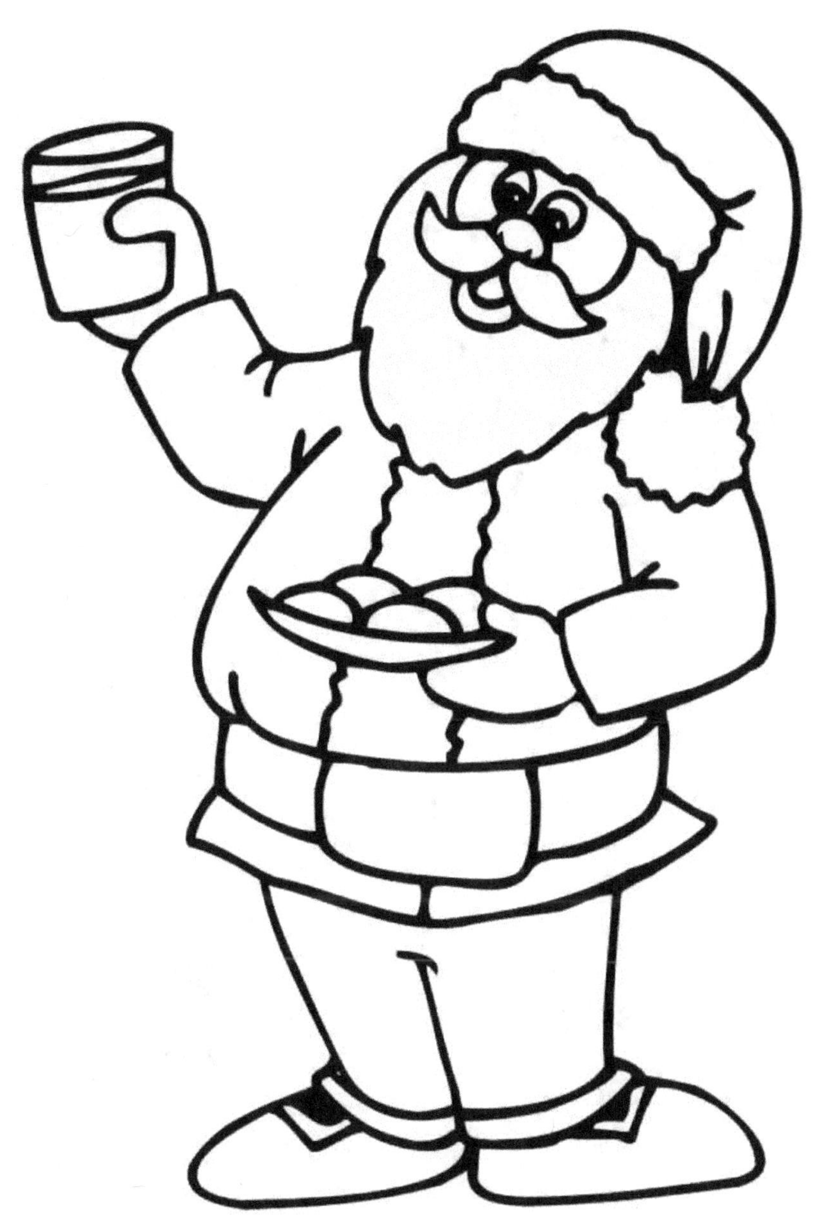

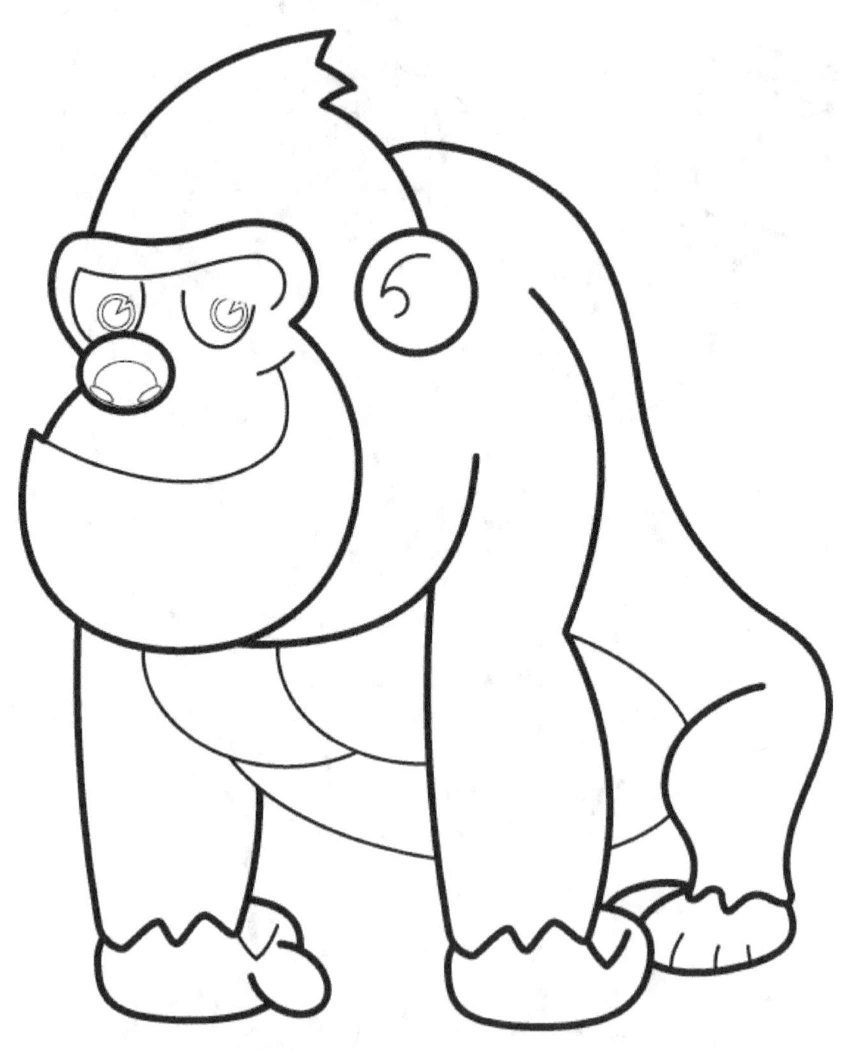

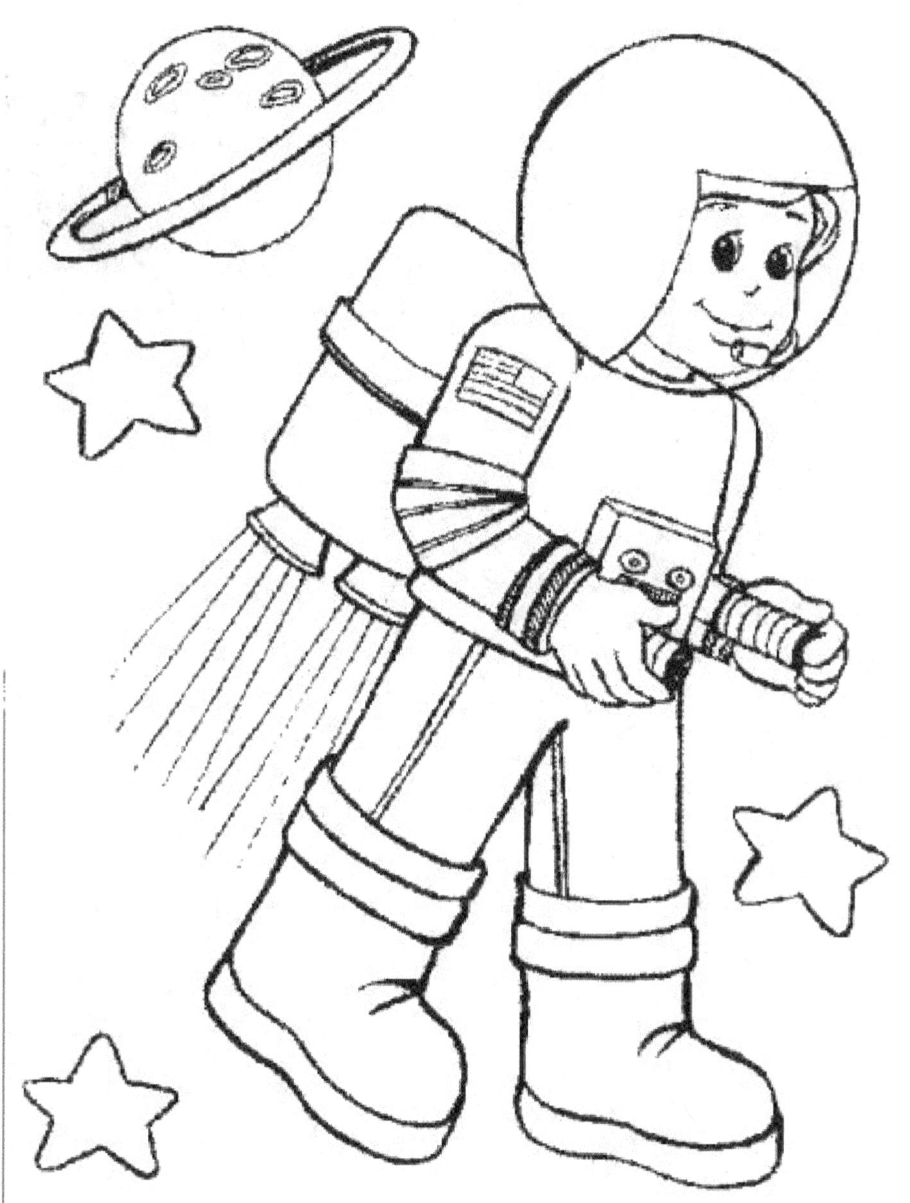

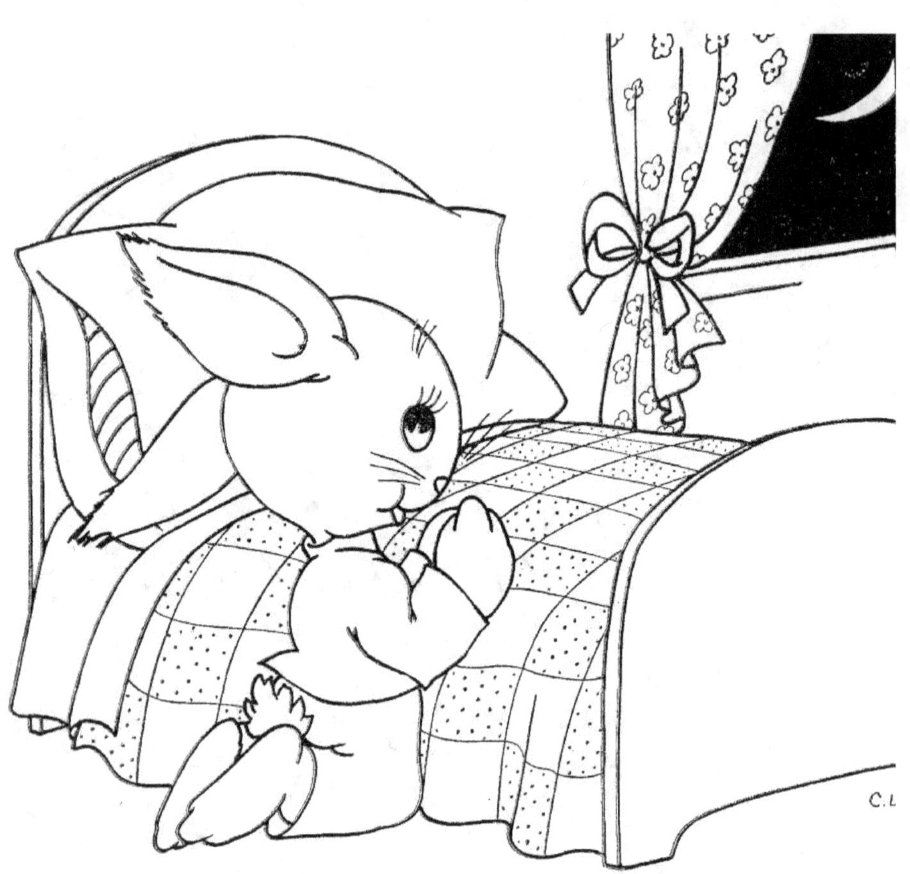

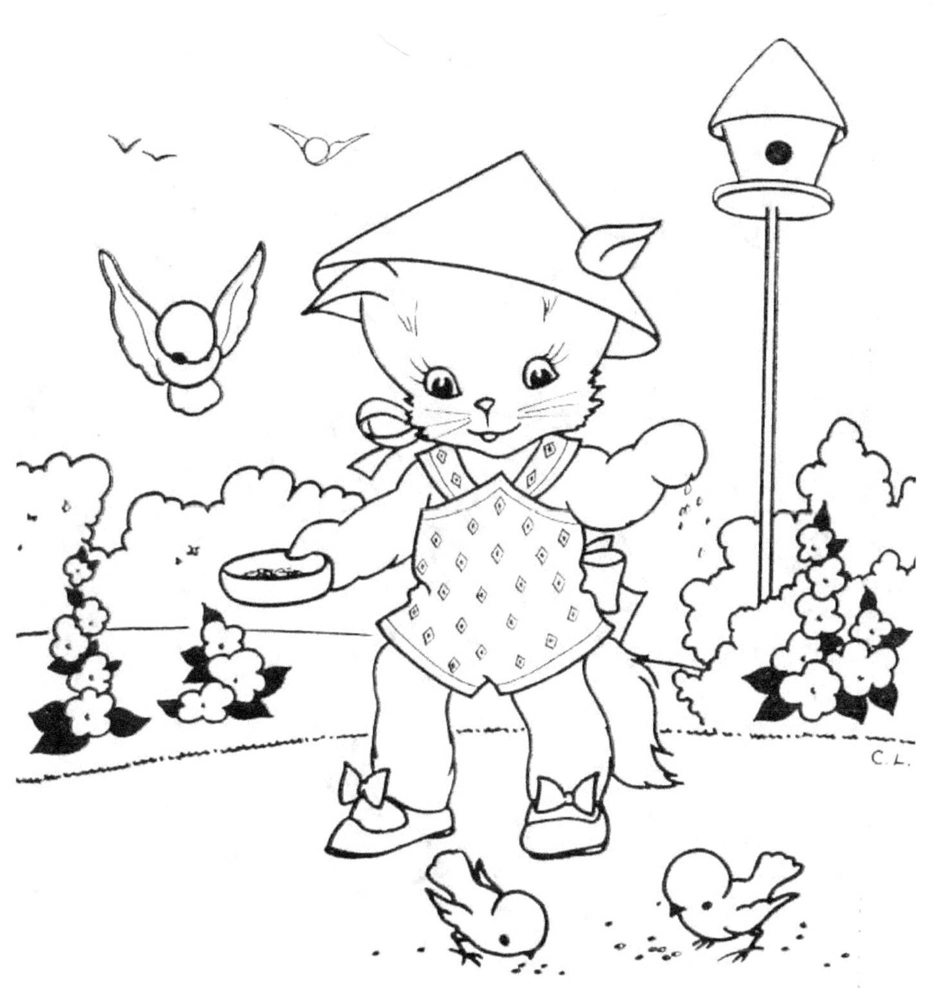

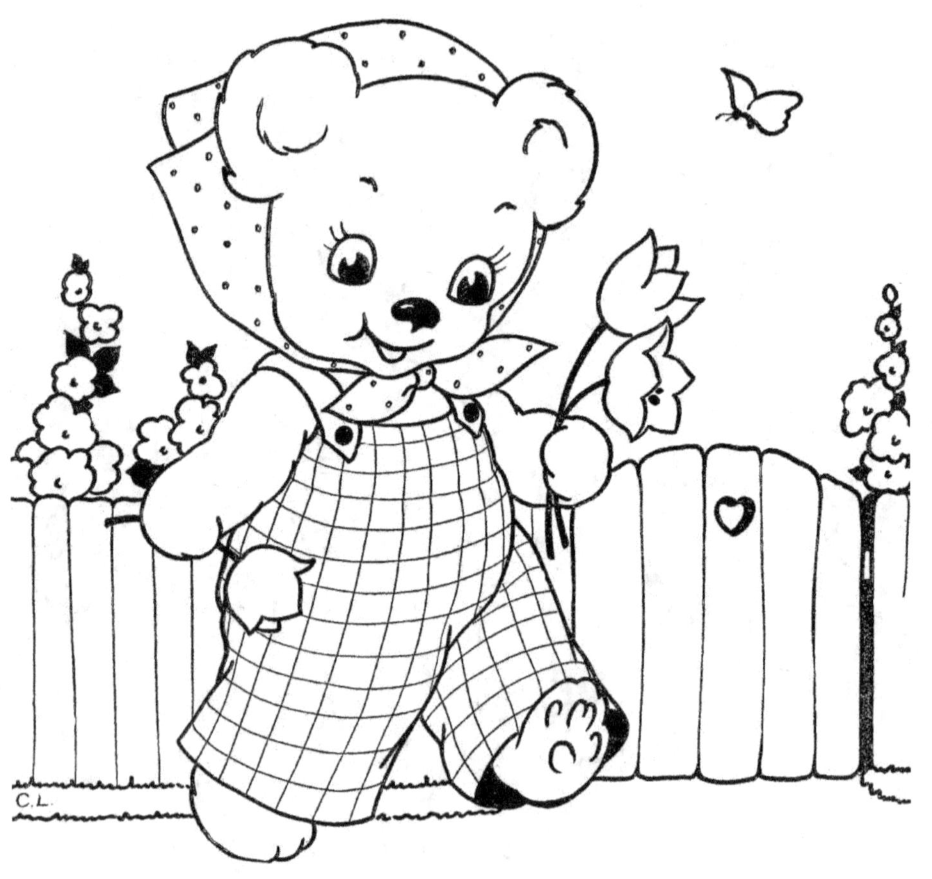

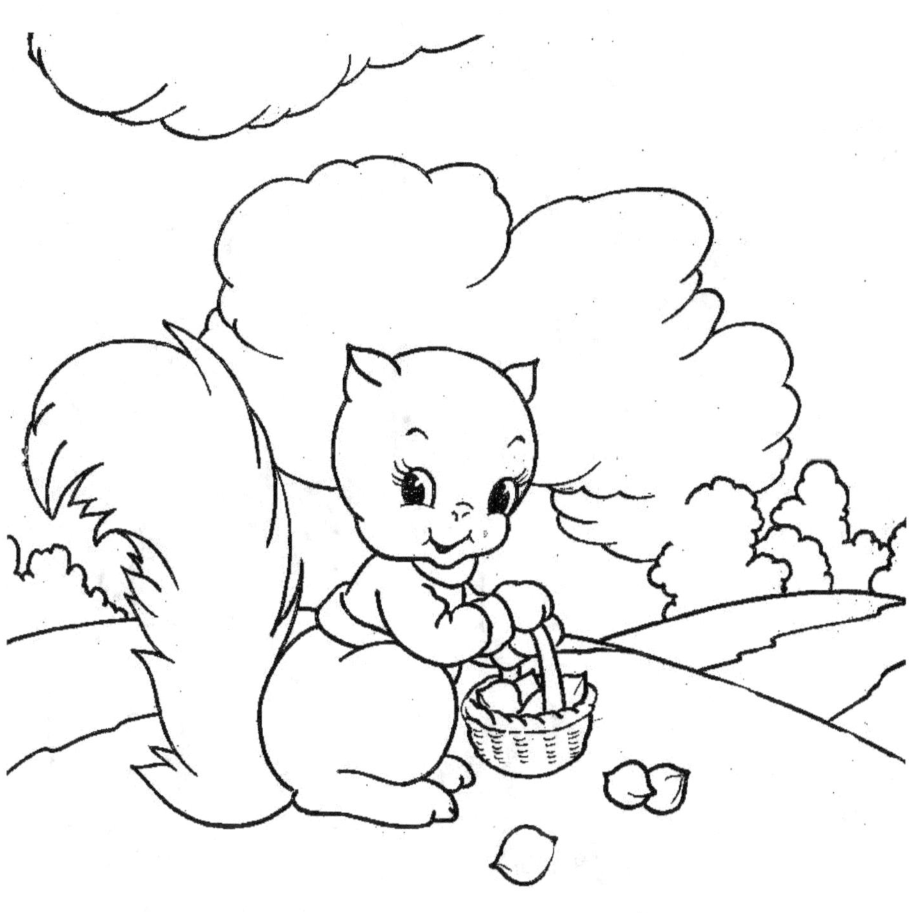

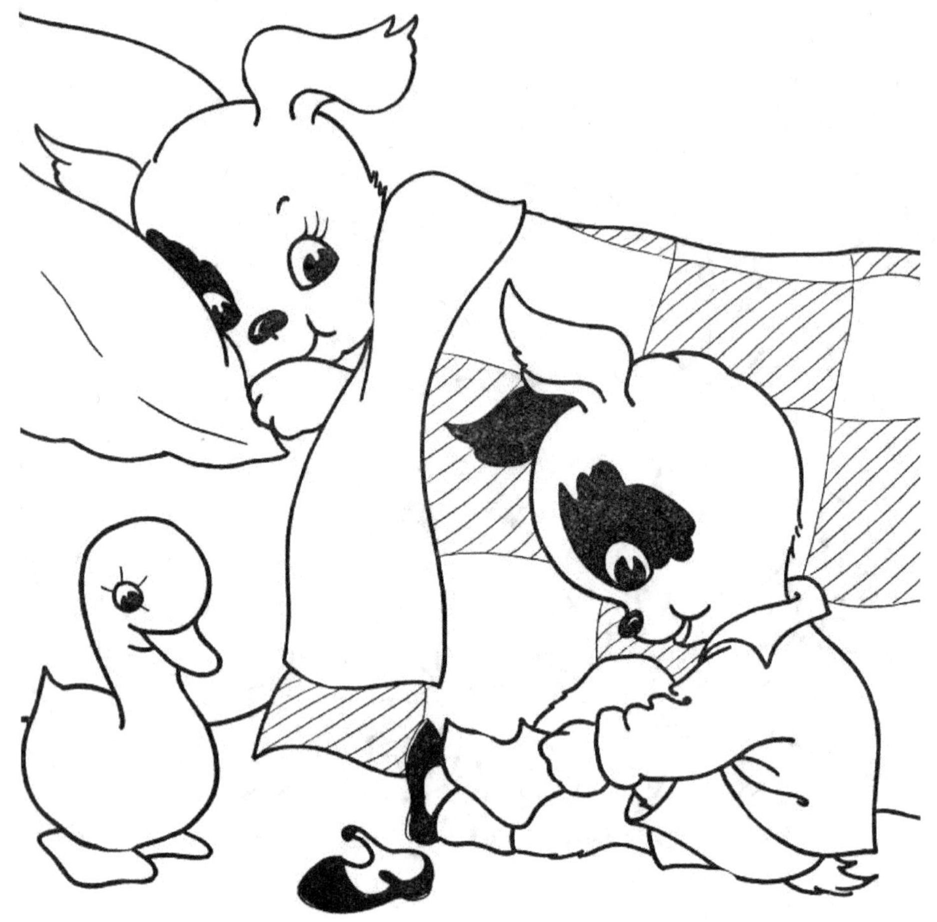

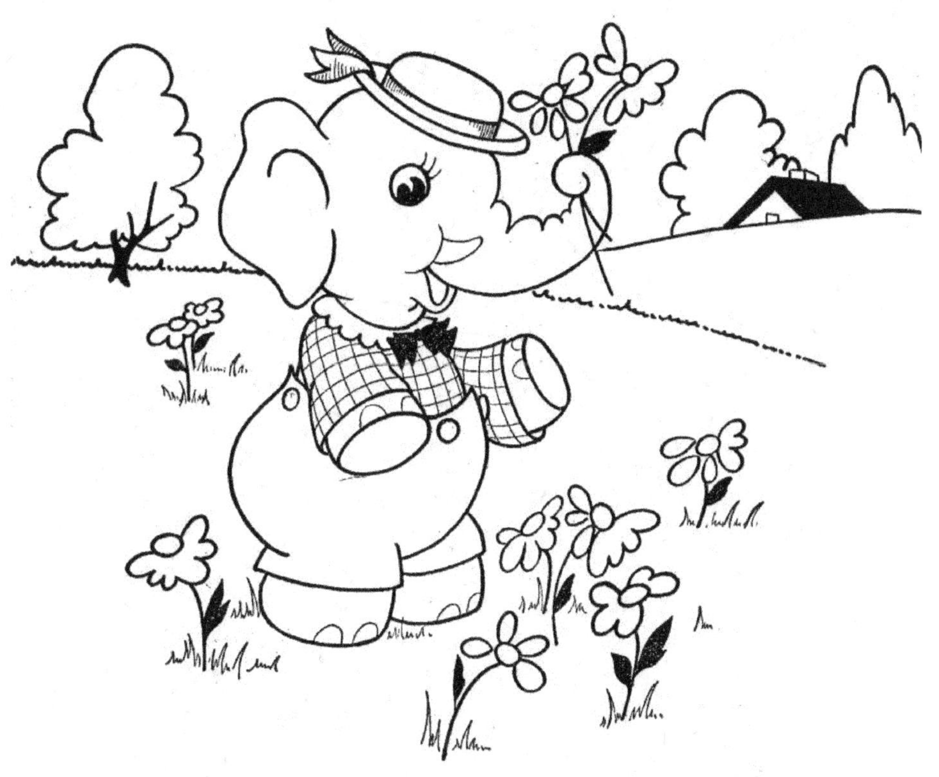

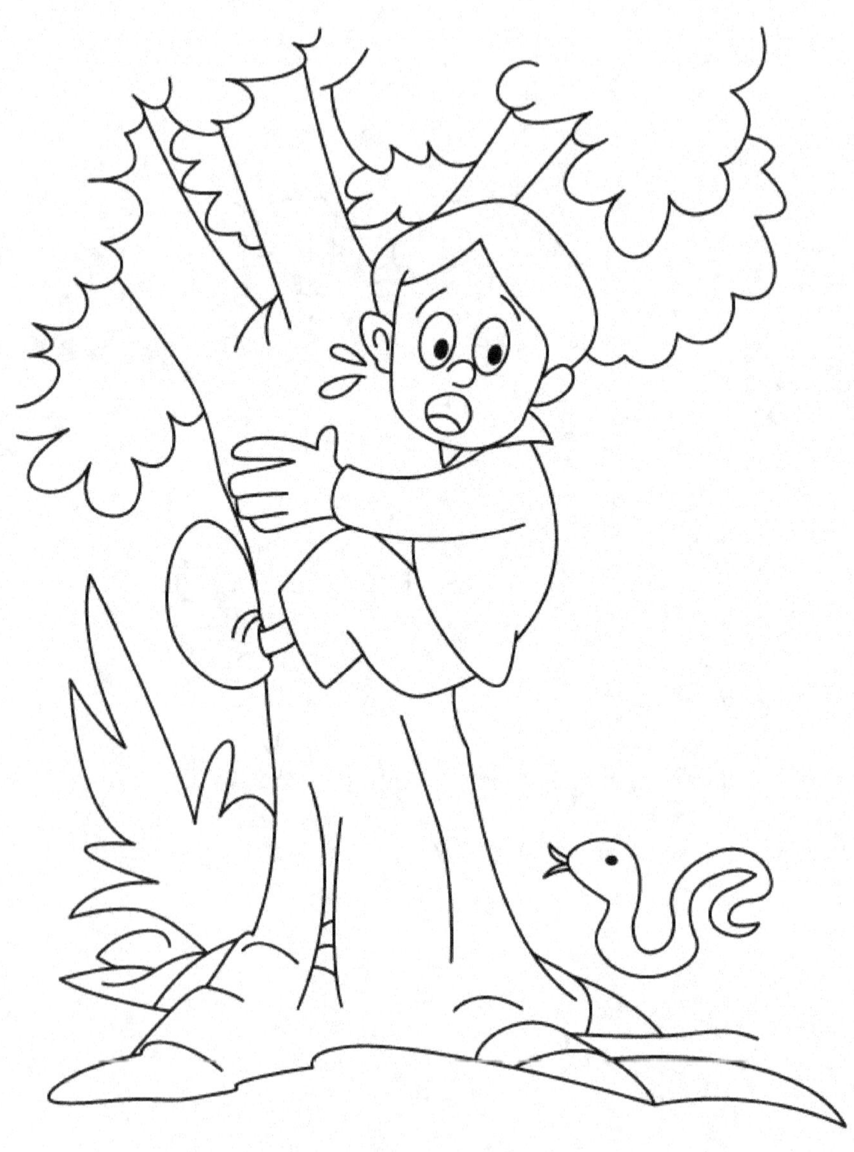

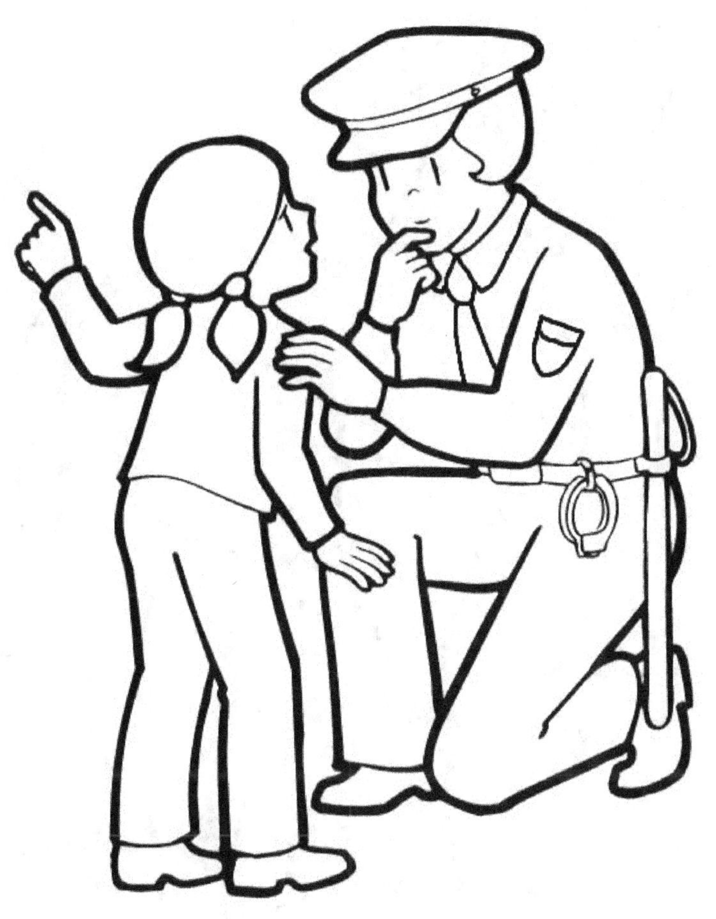

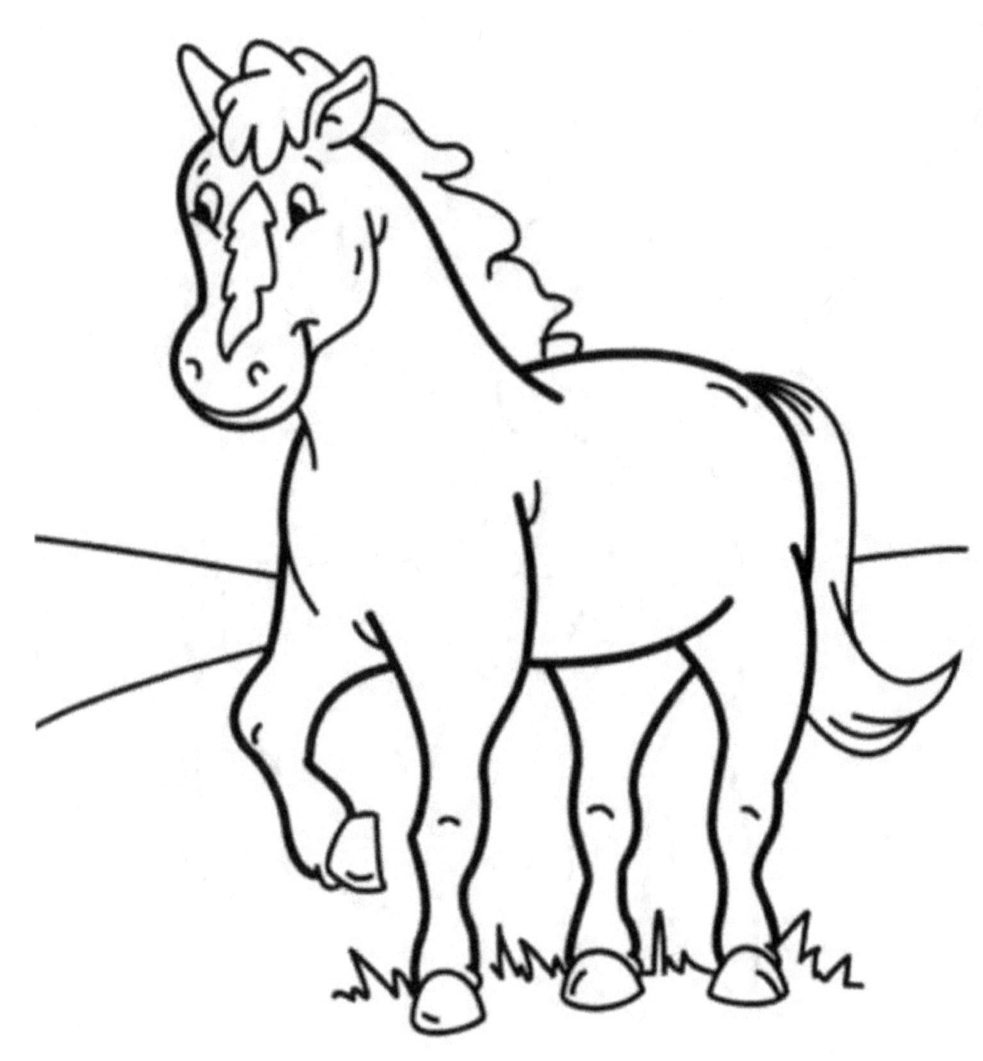

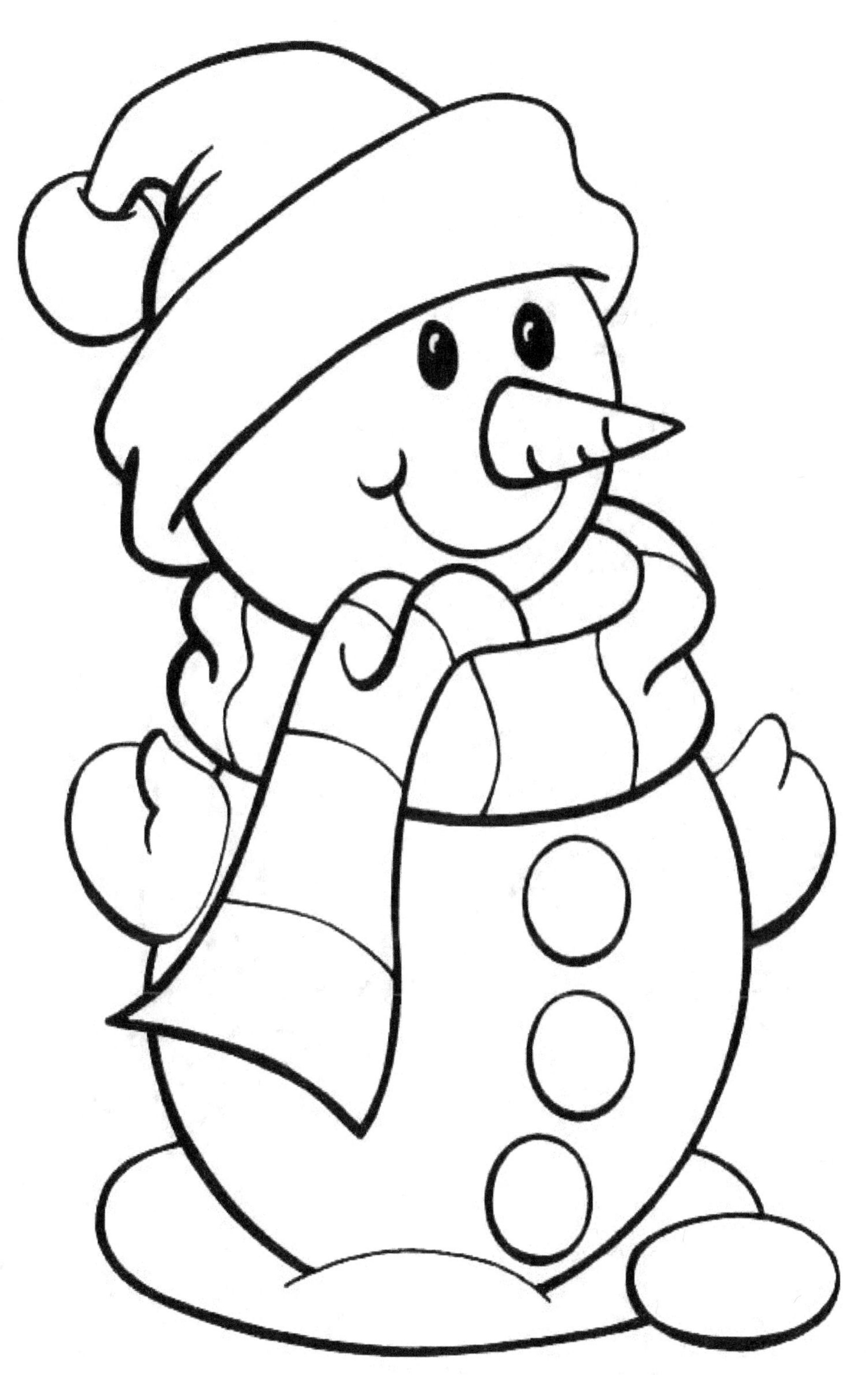

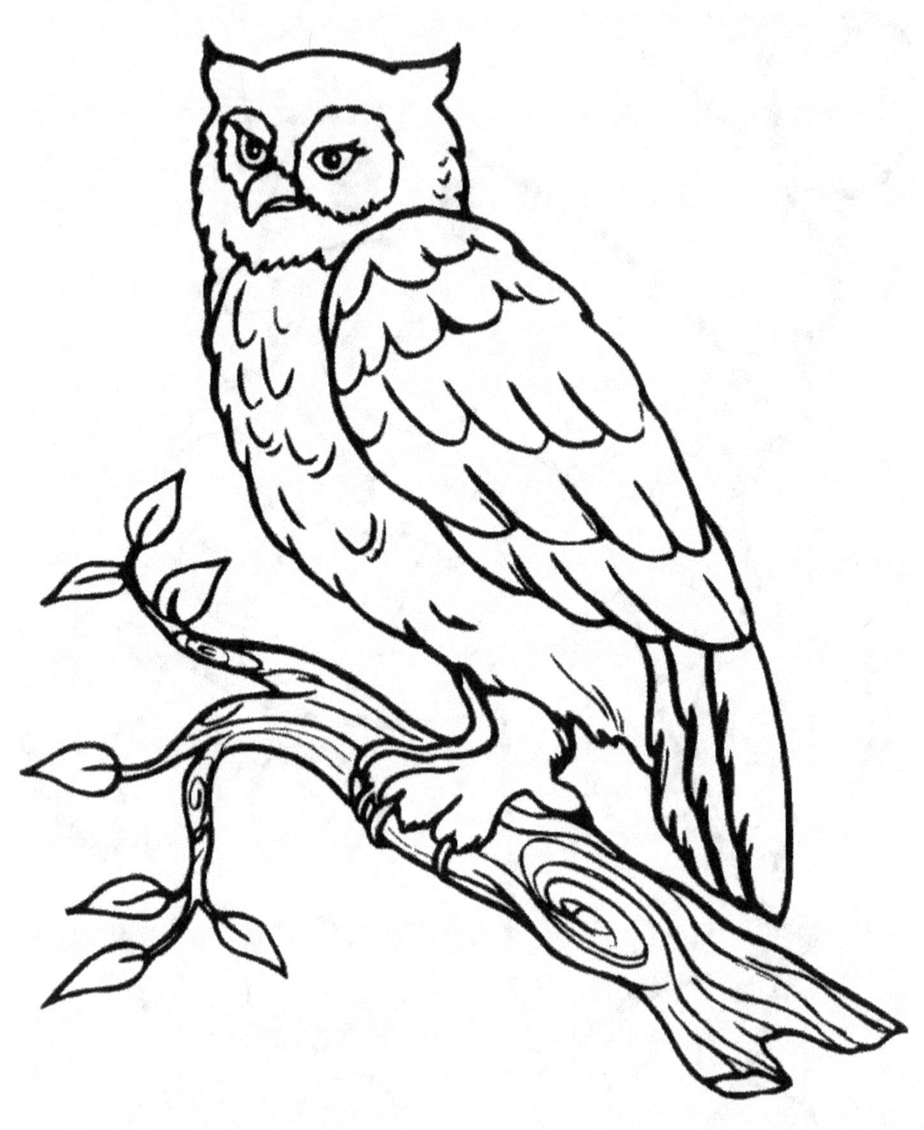

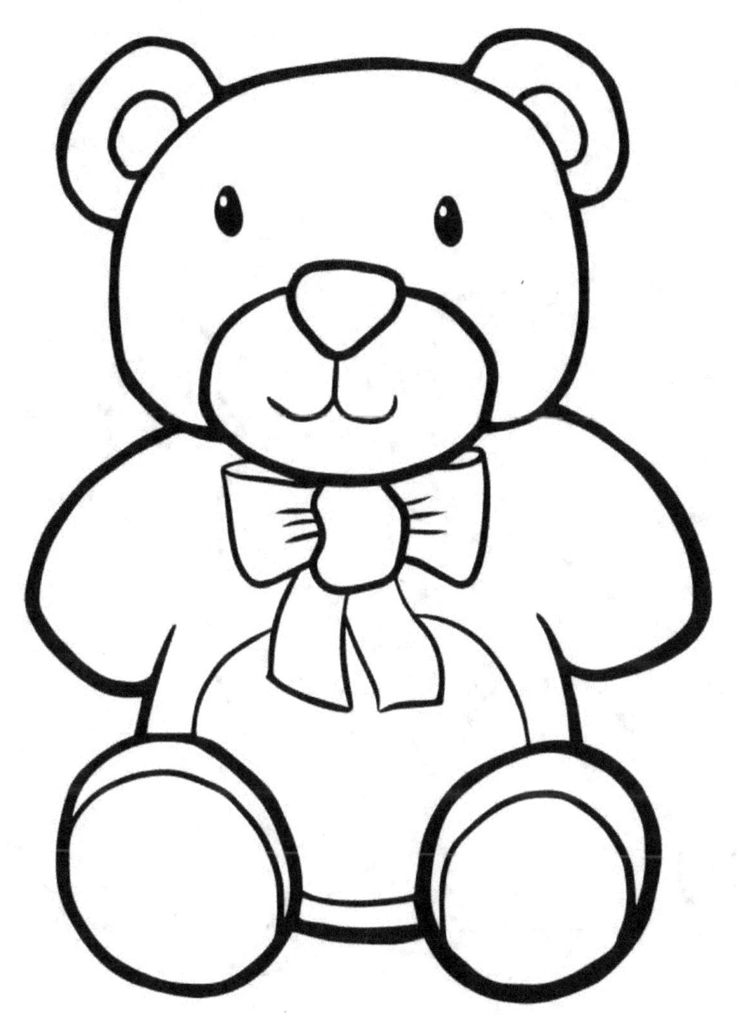

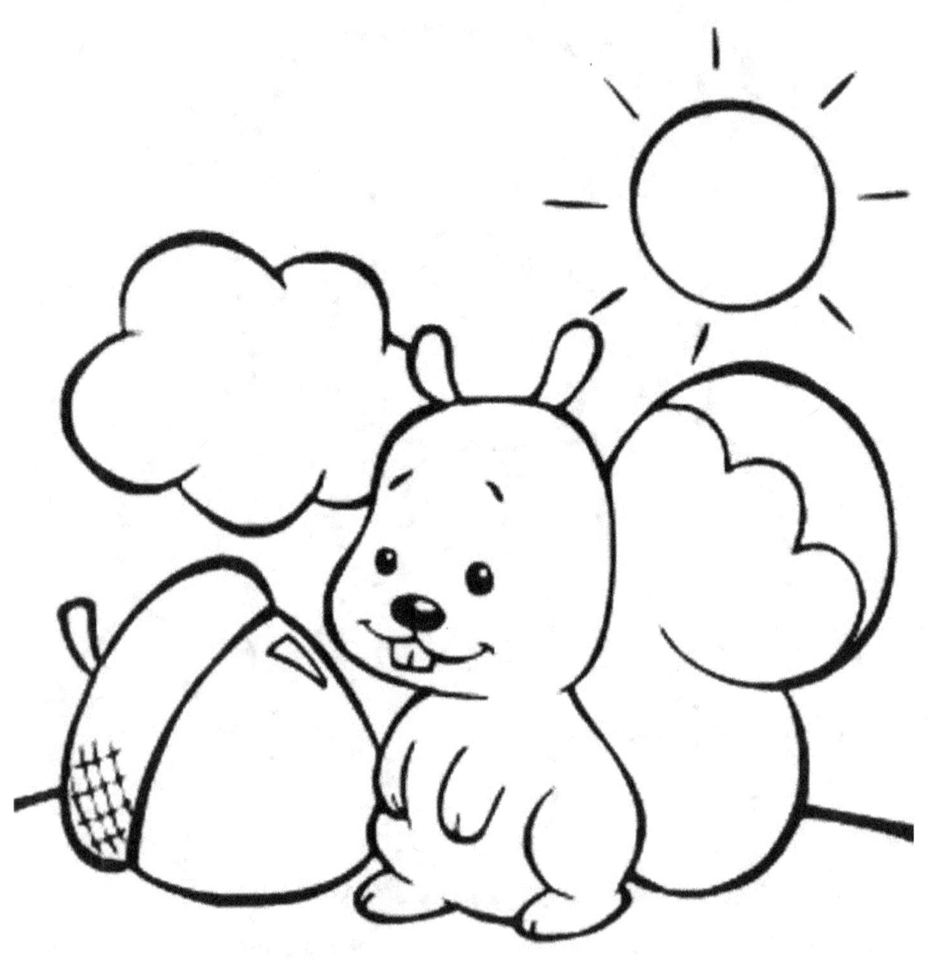

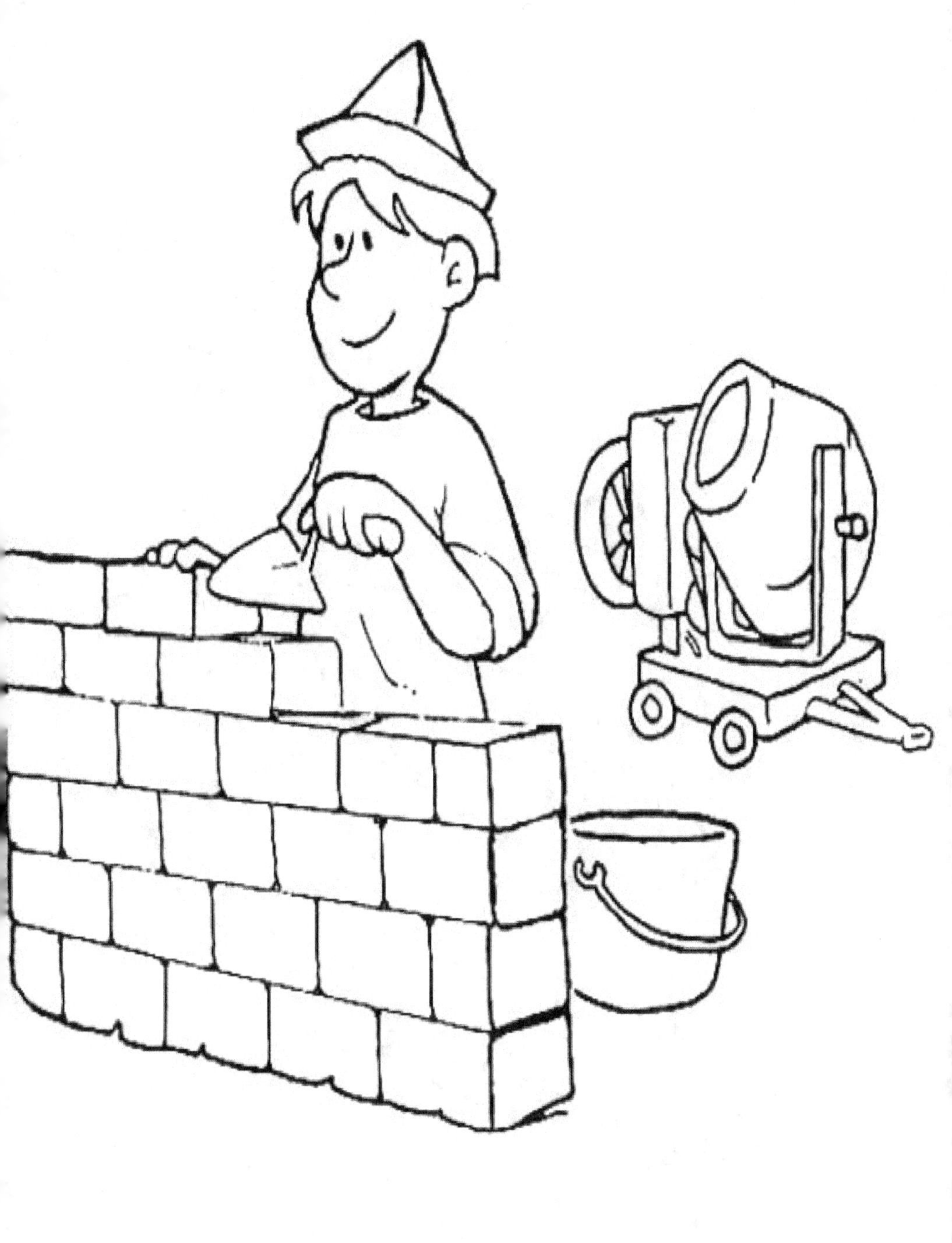

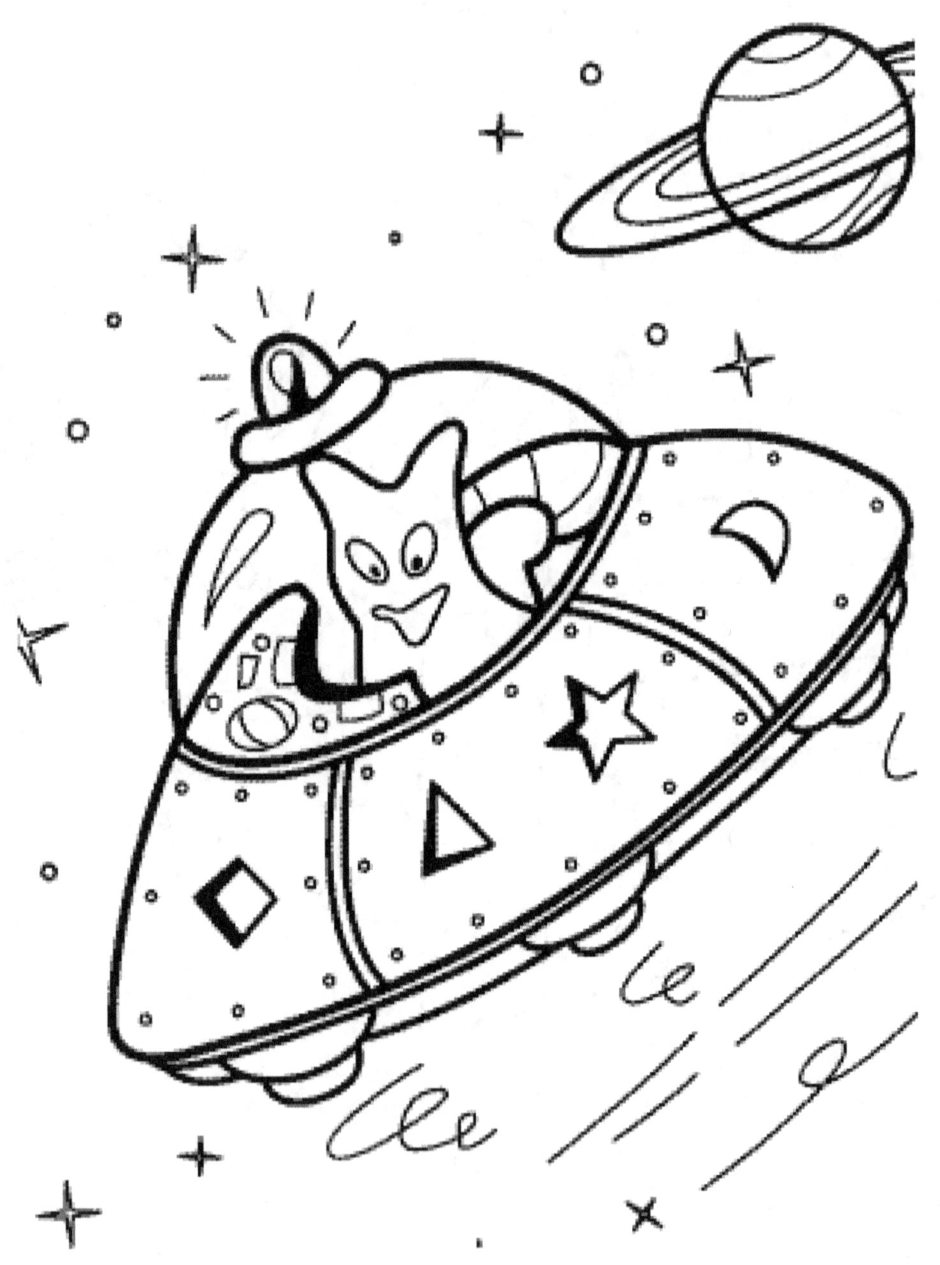

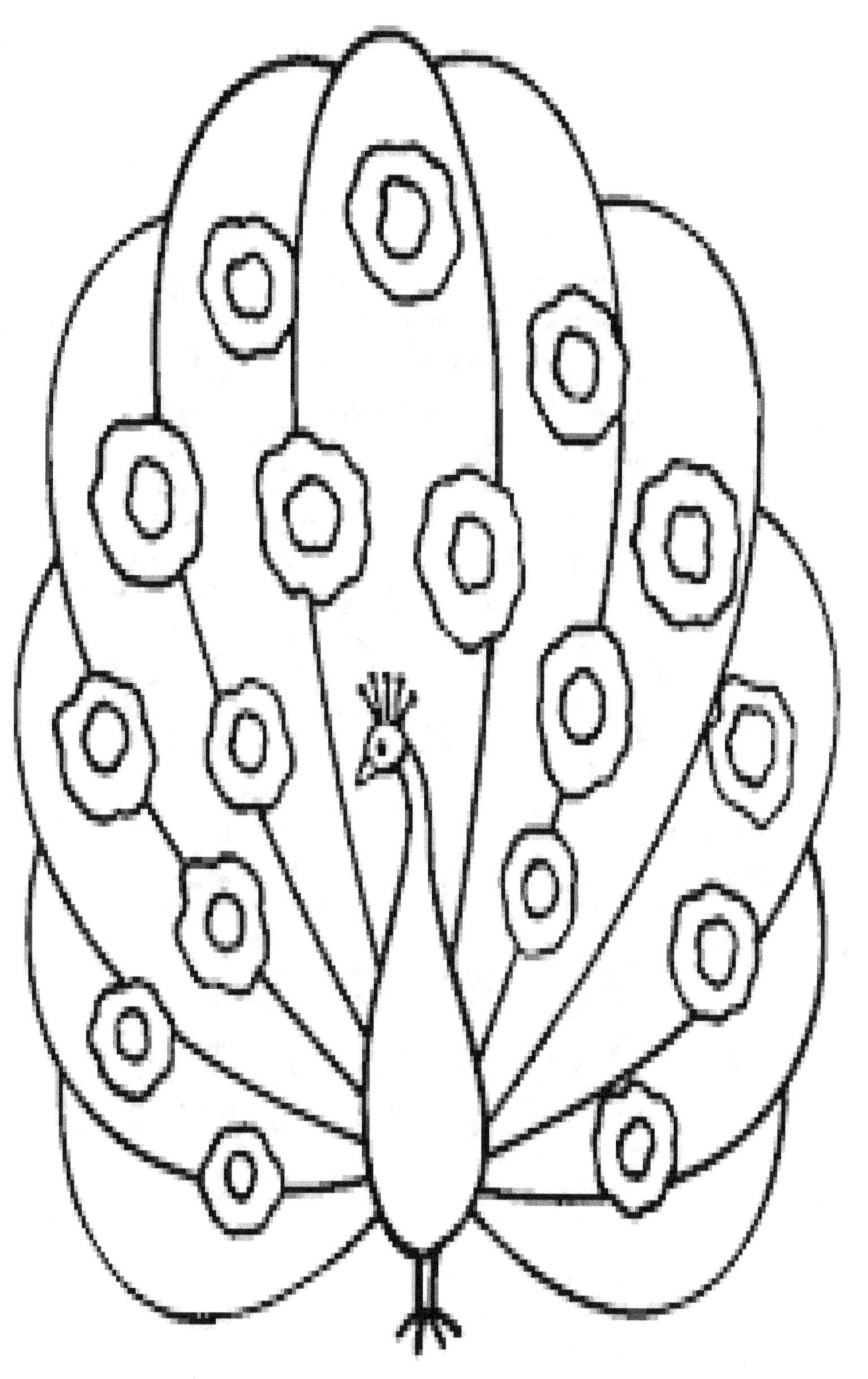

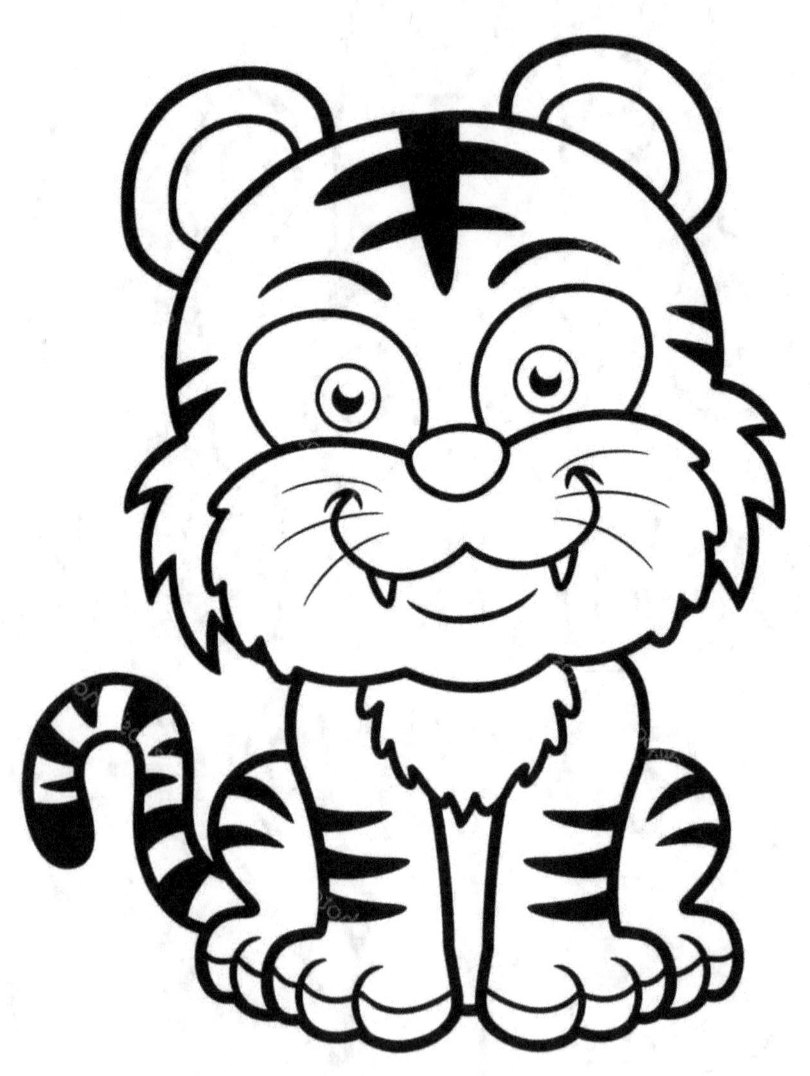

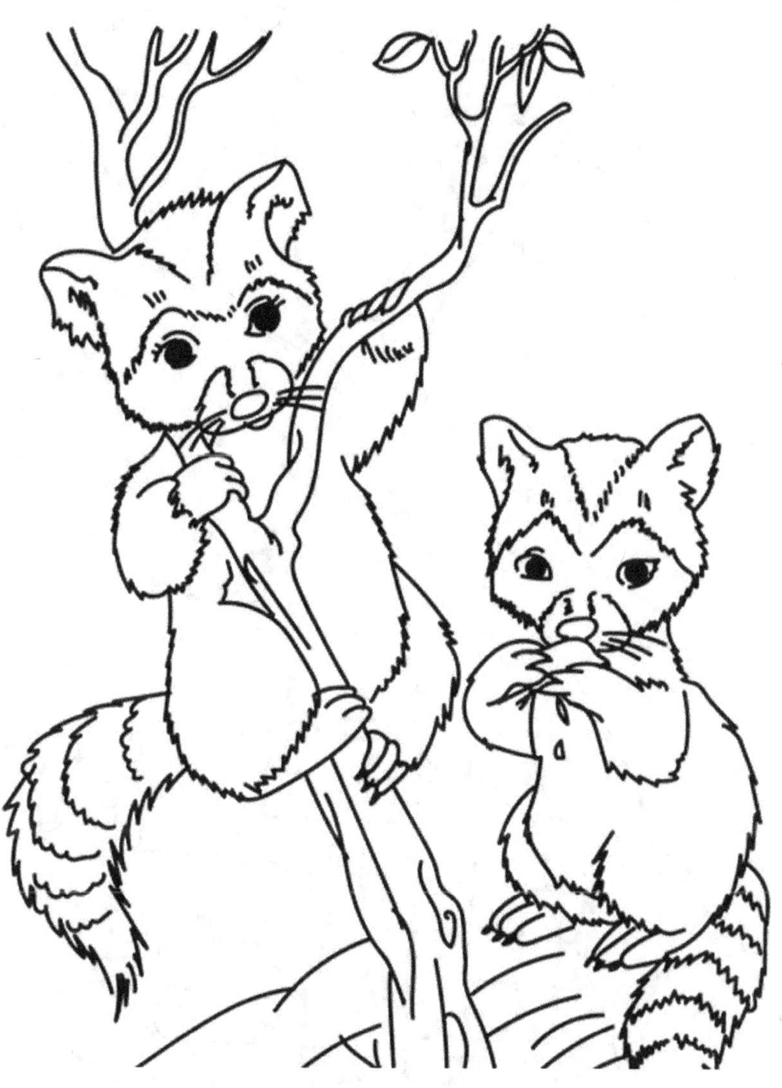

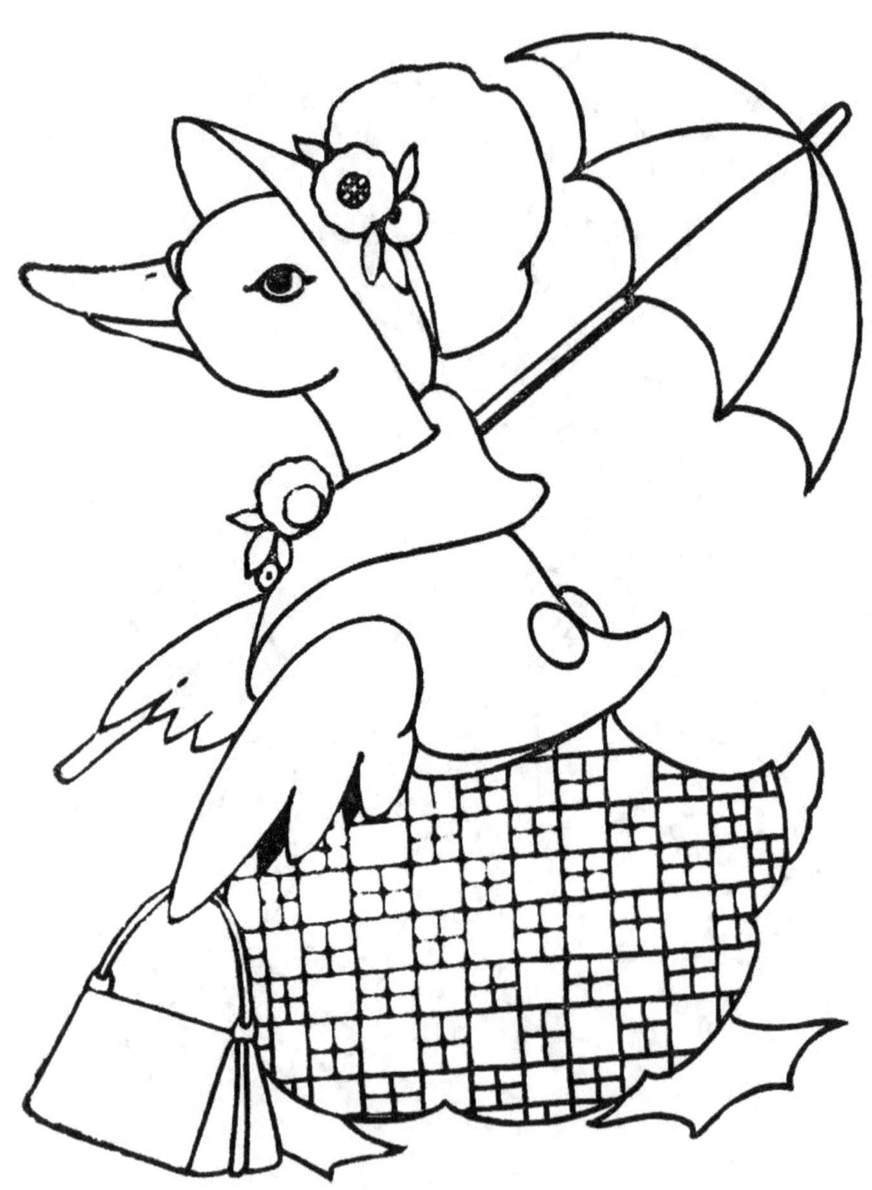

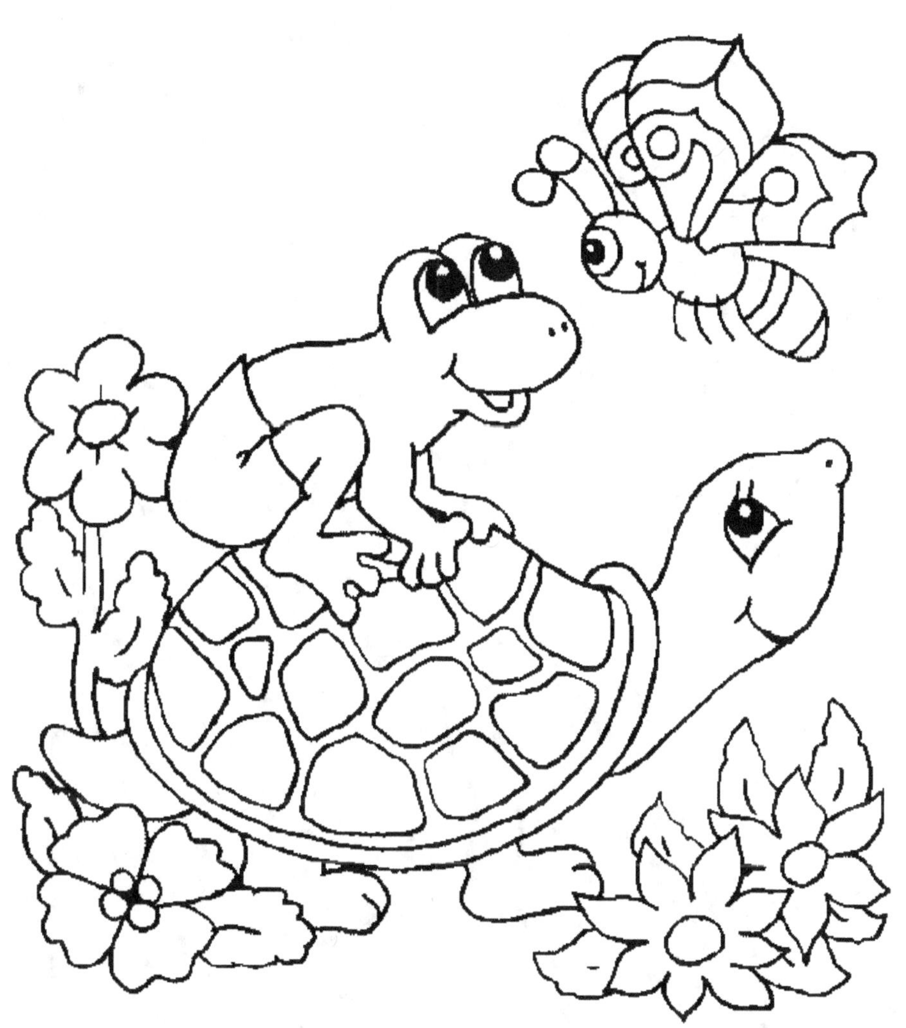

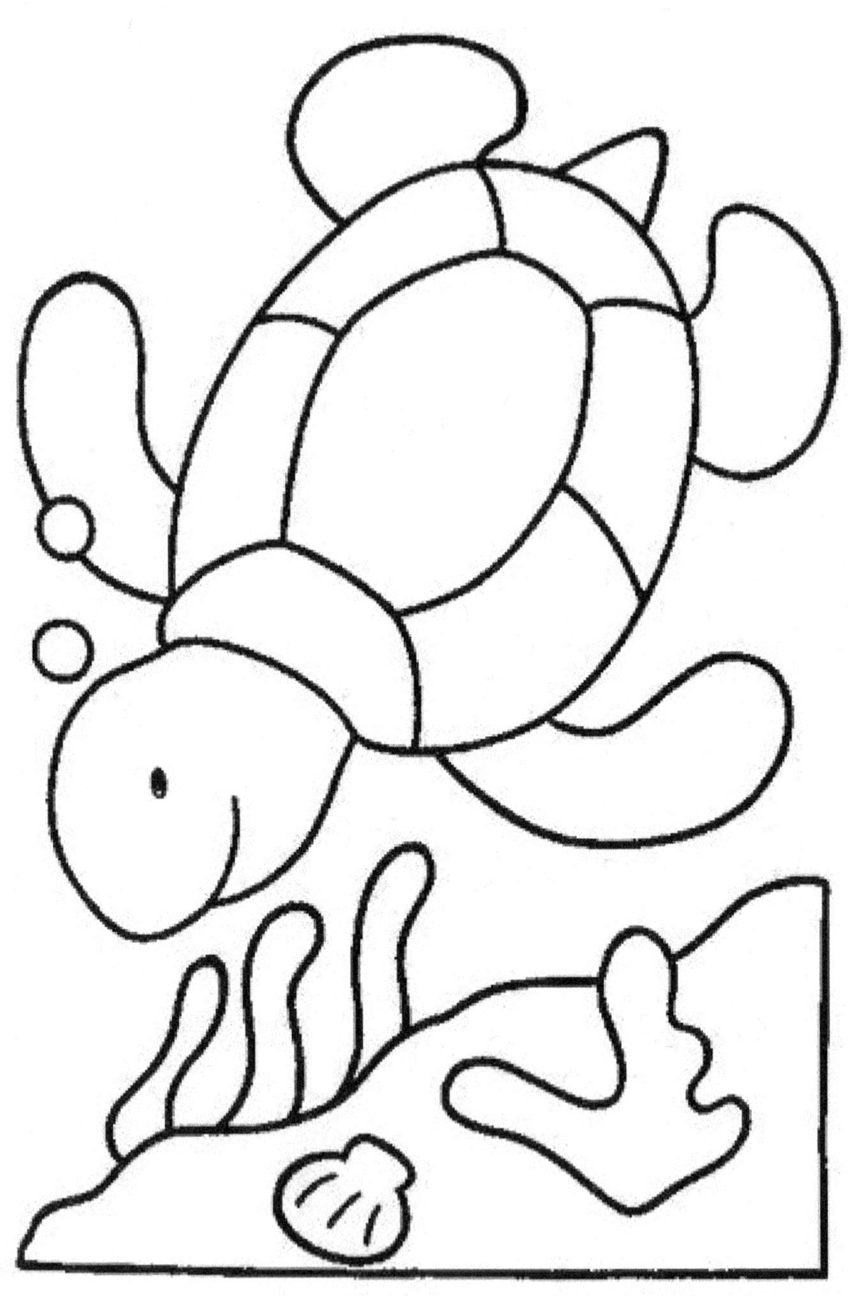

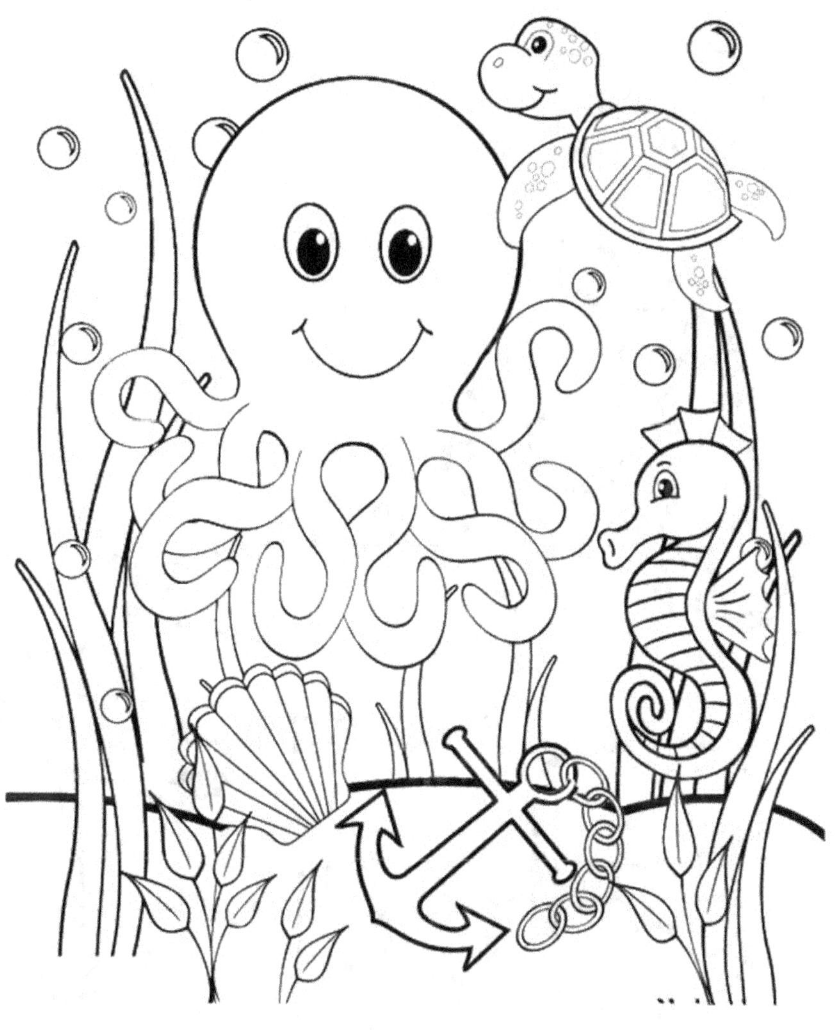

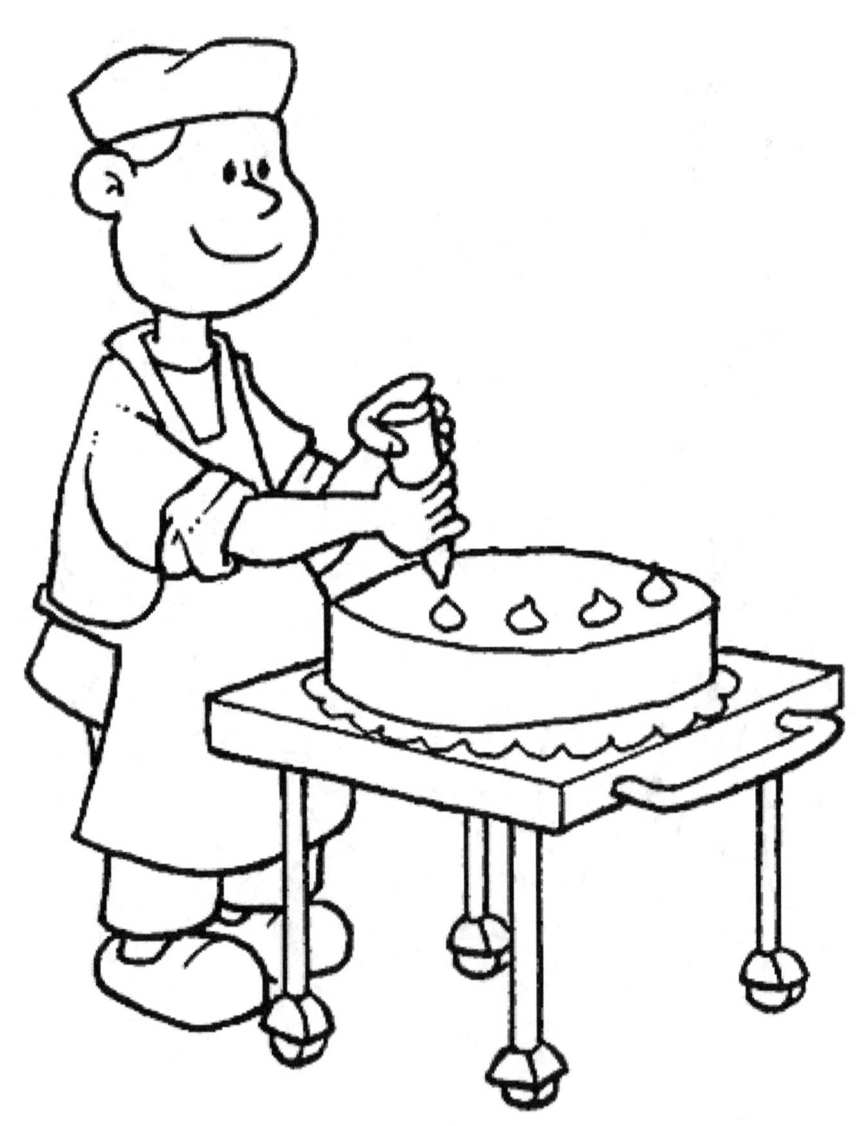